LISTEN
OUT
LOUD

A Life in Music—Managing McCartney,
Madonna, and Michael Jackson

RON WEISNER
with Alan Goldsher

Guilford, Connecticut

An imprint of Rowman & Littlefield

Distributed by NATIONAL BOOK NETWORK

Copyright © 2014 by Ron Weisner
First Lyons Paperback Edition, 2016

All photos courtesy of the author.

British Library Cataloguing in Publication Information Available

The Library of Congress has previously catalogued an earlier (hardcover) edition as follows:

Weisner, Ron author.
  Listen out loud : a life in music—managing McCartney, Madonna, and Michael Jackson / Ron Weisner with Alan Goldsher.
      pages cm
  Includes index.
  ISBN 978-0-7627-9144-6
  1. Weisner, Ron. 2. Sound recording executives and producers—United States—Biography. I. Goldsher, Alan, 1966– author. II. Title.
  ML429.W37A3 2014
  781.64092—dc23
  [B]

                                                                    2014011005

ISBN 978-1-4930-0856-8 (pbk.)
ISBN 978-1-4930-1085-1 (e-book)

♾™ The paper used in this publication meets the minimum requirements of American National Standard for Information Sciences—Permanence of Paper for Printed Library Materials, ANSI/NISO Z39.48-1992.

For my children and grandchildren . . . for going along and never having to put up with a "normal" person, who was gone quite a bit. And to my mom, who recently passed, for always believing in me and encouraging me to achieve my dreams.

CONTENTS

FOREWORD

by Gladys Knight

Let me tell you about Ron Weisner.

Some folks who manage musicians, they'll find an artist and hear some potential, some talent, and a catchy song or two, and they'll want to get on the boat, without much thought as to how they can help the singer rise above everything out there. They'll see dollar signs and will do what they can to squeeze every last cent out of the artist as quickly as possible, often to the detriment of his or her art, career, and life. They think about what they'll do for the artist next week, not next year.

That's not Ron. Ron thinks big picture. In other words, he might suggest you make a musical or personal choice that might not make sense to you in the moment, but if you listen to him and have patience, it'll pay off big for you three years later.

Now Ron, he has a great ear . . . and sure, lots of people have great ears, but Ron's ears can hear the Real Thing. But in Ron's mind, the Real Thing is more than potential, talent, and some nice tunes. The Real Thing is about heart, and kindness, and professionalism. The Real Thing is about striving for perfection, about using your gifts to the best of your abilities. The Real Thing sets you apart from the person who just wants to be famous and make money. And that's why I was so honored to have him as my manager, because I knew Ron saw the other side, the whole package—Gladys the singer *and* Gladys the woman. The passion and loyalty Ron has for his artists, his business associates, and his friends are unmatched.

I tend to believe that people are basically honest, fair, and good, but over the years I learned that some representatives speak to you with a silver tongue, going on and on about what they'll do for you, but, in reality, it's all about what you can do for them. There are countless singers who have had their careers ruined and their bank accounts emptied by those sorts of hucksters. And, sure, Ron wanted to make money for everyone, but it was more important to him that you succeed, both professionally and personally. Trust me, that's rare in a manager.

Now, with the music industry in such flux and turmoil, it's the perfect time for Ron to tell his story. There's a whole new generation of representatives, producers, and executives who could stand to learn from his experience. And if they take what he has to say to heart, maybe, just maybe, they can make our entertainment world a little bit better.

INTRODUCTION

Michael Jackson's issues with prescription drugs began in 1983, after he was horribly burned during an accident on the set of a Pepsi commercial. He was prescribed pain medication to help him deal with the burns on his head; considering his addictive personality, I wasn't surprised when he got hooked.

As is probably the case with most any celebrity, Michael never had any problem getting meds; he had several acquaintances who I liked to call "concierge doctors," quacks who would dole out any drug that Michael asked for, any time he wanted. His inner circle was no help. Almost immediately after I was fired, Michael surrounded himself with yes-men who didn't have the balls to tell Michael that he needed to clean up. Instead of stepping up and trying to help their benefactor, they facilitated him.

There were other people in Michael's life who attempted interventions, none of whom came close to helping. Whenever I tried to discuss the drug situation, he immediately tuned out and moved on to another topic. His sister LaToya, a nice lady whose horrible reputation was, to me, exaggerated, was the only person in the family who consistently tried to help Michael and had the same experience. "He doesn't want to deal with it," she told me. "Whenever I say something about it, he gets upset and walks out of the room."

"You guys are dealing with it all wrong," I said. "You're making a big mistake. If it was my brother, I'd snatch him.

I'd get some people to grab him, take him to some rehab facility in the middle of nowhere, and stay with him until he was okay. But he doesn't want to hear about it, and he doesn't want to deal with it, so stop *asking*, and start *doing*. That's the only option."

By the time 2006 rolled around, I'd had some version of this conversation with LaToya at least ten times. *At least.*

Unless you knew Michael when he was on, you might not have been able to notice the effects of the drugs. To me, Michael on drugs was a shadow of his sober self, and even after the way he dumped me, I still cared about the guy—I couldn't help it—so I called LaToya and told her, "Let's do this. Let's get him fixed. I'll put together a team, I'll arrange for an airplane, I'll find the right facility. I'll put everything in place, and pay for it myself. You don't have to do anything except to tell me exactly where he's going to be at the appointed day and time."

LaToya gave me the go-ahead, and I began making plans. But that wasn't as easy as it might've been had Michael been in the country.

His situation had escalated so badly that he escaped to Bahrain, where Prince Abdullah Hamad Al Khalifa provided Michael with the cash he needed to maintain the lifestyle to which he'd become accustomed. Worst of all, the sheik's star-fucking son was making sure he had all the drugs he wanted. Had Michael been in LA, I could've set it all up with one quick phone call, but with him on the other side of the world, it took months of calls and thousands of dollars.

On May 15, two days before the kidnapping—and yes, that's exactly what this was, a kidnapping—I got a call from LaToya, who was, to put it mildly, freaking out. *"You gotta stop it you gotta stop it you gotta stop it!"*

I let her go on in this vein for a minute or three, then interrupted her: "LaToya, it's not that easy. It took a lot of work to set it up, and it'll take even more work to call it off."

"I don't care! You gotta stop it you gotta stop it you gotta stop it."

She seemed more than a little unhinged, and I was frankly afraid of what would happen if I refused—she might mention my plan to the wrong person, who'd mention it to another wrong person, and I'd be screwed. So I stopped it all: The airplane, the rehab facility, the team, everything came to a halt. It cost me more money than I'd care to admit, a couple of friendships, and a business relationship or two, but I pulled the plug. In retrospect, it was probably for the best because, as one of my attorneys pointed out, there was little question that John Law would view this as a kidnapping, rather than an attempt to help a colleague, and kidnapping, lest we forget, is a federal crime. (The lawyer wasn't too concerned, though: "You gotta do what you gotta do," he said. "Just don't assassinate anybody.")

I don't know if the snatching—or the kidnapping, or whatever you want to call it—would've lengthened Michael's life. I don't know if it would've made him a happier, more productive person. But at the very least, it would've given him a chance.

CHAPTER ONE

Buddah

We were the renegades, the psychos, the nut cases.
But we got it done.

I've always listened to music, because, as far as I knew, that's what you did. And thanks to a lucky roll of the geographical dice, when I was a kid, I heard *everything*.

What kind of music you first listen to is usually based on your environment. If the guy who lives in the apartment to the left of yours plays his Charlie Parker and Ella Fitzgerald records all the time, you might well develop an affinity for jazz. If the girl who lives in the apartment on the right plays Muddy Waters and Leadbelly, you'll probably dig the blues. If you were like me, and you grew up in a place like the Williamsburg section of Brooklyn, whose population covered all races, creeds, and colors, you heard everything, and you liked everything.

No one in the building where my family lived had air conditioning, so during the summer, practically everyone who lived there spent their days outside, where each afternoon was a sonic carnival: While the fire hydrant was spitting out streams of cool water, cars drove by with their windows open and their radios blaring Elvis; our neighbors put their speakers in their window facing out and turned up the volume on their Ike and Tina Turner records; the Jamaicans in the building next door played calypso jams on their transistor radios. And everyone danced in the streets to whatever song was loudest. In the grand scheme of things, living in such close proximity to all of these music obsessives—and having access to all those diverse sounds—offered me a better education than any schooling. This atmosphere helped me understand well before I would have otherwise that there were many different people in this country, and different people meant different cultures, and different cultures meant different music.

As I matured, so did my ears, and I developed more specific likes. The releases from Motown Records in Detroit, for instance, were about as good as it got. You had the Temptations and the Four Tops harmonizing like there was no tomorrow. You had Smokey Robinson and the Miracles helping you learn about love. You had Marvin Gaye teaching you every single meaning of the word *soul*. Outside of Detroit, you had the Memphis mafia, the Stax records roster, with Wilson Pickett, Otis Redding, and Albert King. And we can't forget James Brown and Aretha Franklin, who were ballsier and sweatier than all of 'em. The one common factor about the sounds heard throughout Williamsburg was the attitude, and that attitude was *uplifting*. There wasn't any negativity, or anger, or depression, or nastiness. No hardcore, no rage. Just fun. It was a daily dance party.

My parents bought me a cheap little turntable, on which I played my 45 RPMs, my early favorites being the dynamic

A/B single James Brown's "Papa's Got a Brand New Bag" and "I Feel Good." I was always hustling just to get a couple of bucks so I could afford to buy more music, and, for me, hustling meant a daily trip up and down the street to pick up the empty Rheingold and Schaffer beer bottles from the empty porches, then redeeming them at the nearby grocery store. I'd get a nickel a bottle, which went a long way. Most of the money went toward music, but on Saturdays, if I hadn't bought a record or three during the week, I'd hit the local movie theater where, for fifty cents, I could watch three movies, one right after the other. Some of the movies were good, and some were bad, but the air conditioning was always great.

We moved to Jamaica, Queens when I was twelve, to a house situated between the Kennedy and LaGuardia Airports. While a perfectly nice area, it was lacking Brooklyn's party vibe, and because none of our neighbors played music loudly enough for me to hear, I had to do what everyone else did when they wanted to hear new sounds: listen to the radio. My first stop was always WLIB, the biggest R&B station in New York. Based in Harlem, they spent much of their in-between-song talk time discussing the artists who were coming to the Apollo Theater, and, man, I wanted in.

Over the last however many years, I've produced dozens of shows at the Apollo, featuring everyone from Stevie Wonder, to Aretha Franklin, to James Brown. And at some point during each and every one of these gigs, I'll look up to the back of the second balcony and remember when the room was once my second home.

Okay, that's a slight exaggeration: The Apollo wasn't my second home, but in the mid- and late 1960s, it was damn

My favorite . . . Ella Fitzgerald

close. It was there I fell in love with Aretha Franklin. It was there I saw Marvin Gaye transcend time and space. It was there I saw James Brown, which was a religious experience. It was there I saw the Ike and Tina Turner Review melt the girders. It was there I saw Stevie Wonder when he was still Little Stevie Wonder, doing unimaginable things on his harmonica. It was there that Count Basie and Ella Fitzgerald introduced me to the joys of live jazz.

There were usually three or four acts that preceded the headliner, groups like the Marvelettes, the Crystals, and the van Dykes, folks that had a hit, maybe two, but they were always good. It was an entertaining night of music, and that always stayed in my head; I imagined that if I ever got involved with the music world, I'd want to make certain that if you shelled out your two, or five, or ten, or fifty bucks, you'd walk away feeling like you'd received more than your money's worth. (Excuse me if I sound like a cranky old guy for a minute, but back then, the stage would be crowded with horn and string players; today, it'll just be a guy and his laptop. Also, when I first started regularly visiting Las Vegas, every hotel had a house band. Now it's Cirque de Vegas, replete with pre-recorded background vocals and instrumental tracks. If you see a Vegas show in which the act is actually every note that's allegedly coming out of their mouths, consider yourself lucky. There's a whole generation of listeners who haven't experienced what it's like to see a tight, well-rehearsed band blow the roof off a theater, and it breaks my heart that today it's considered a successful show when the prerecorded vocal track to which the singer is lip-synching doesn't crap out in the middle of a song. Okay, rant over. Back to our regularly scheduled program.) I guess the Apollo was less of a home, and more of a place of worship, and it rarely cost more than two bucks a ticket. Taking everything into account—the brilliant music, the electric atmosphere, the low cost—I consider many of those shows among the best I've ever seen. *Ever.*

Had my parents known how often I took the train up to Harlem for a night of R&B, they probably wouldn't have been pleased, to say the least. I was generally the only white person in the audience, in part because none of my friends were brave enough to head uptown with me. I'd hear an ad for a James Brown show on the radio, then call one of my pals and say, "J.B. is playing at the Apollo. Let's go!"

They'd say, "No way. Frankie Valli's playing at the Paramount Theater in Brooklyn. Me and the guys are going there."

Now there was certainly nothing wrong with Frankie Valli, but come on, we're talking *James Brown*. "What're you, crazy?"

"It's gonna be a great show!"

"Yeah, well James Brown will be a religious experience." (I didn't actually say that because I didn't know you could equate music with religion in that manner. But had I known, that's what I would've said.)

I could understand their trepidation. There was a period earlier in the century, specifically the 1920s and 1930s, when Harlem was a thriving section of the city for blacks, both culturally and socially. But by the time I started frequenting the area, it had gone downhill, on its way to being completely overrun by crime and drugs. It wasn't dangerous yet, but it wasn't *not* dangerous, if you get my drift. On the surface, it might not have seemed like a great idea to travel up there—*especially* all by myself, *especially* late at night—but save for a few brown-bag drunks calling me a honky, I never had any hassles, and if I had it to do over again, I'd have spent even more time at the Apollo.

So did hearing all these sounds compel me to play an instrument? Absolutely not. Did I want a job in which I could sell, manufacture, or promote music? I didn't even consider it. Did I want to get on the radio and play my favorite songs for the masses? No way. I listened, and listening was enough.

After four years of showing up and doing what I had to do, I graduated. Like most parents, my mother and father wanted me to go to college, but college wasn't me. I figured since I didn't want to be a doctor or a lawyer, I could make something happen on my own. I didn't know what I wanted to do or who I wanted to be, but I doubted that four more years of education—and expensive education at that—would help me make that decision.

For the next few months, I scoured the want ads, and found little that I was qualified for, or wanted to do. I let it be known that I was looking for *anything*, and soon, one of my school friends had an uncle who worked for an advertising agency. I didn't have dreams of being an ad man, but it was better than the alternative—which was sitting at home being glared at by my father—so I had him ask his uncle if there were any openings. His uncle didn't know of any available positions, but he heard through the grapevine that there was a record place that needed someone to work in the mailroom.

I had no idea what "record place" meant. A store? A label? A studio? But it was a job, so I went for an interview. The so-called record place was in Manhattan, in a thirty-plus-floor skyscraper on 6th Avenue and 55th Street. It was called MGM Records.

One of the five major labels of its era, MGM had been around since the late 1940s and had recorded everyone from Erroll Garner, to Connie Francis, to Harry James, to Eartha Kitt, to Roy Orbison, to Hank Williams. They also had, under their umbrella, Verve Records, one of the most prestigious jazz labels of that or any era. MGM Records was a multimillion-dollar company, but I didn't know anything about that; to me, MGM meant movie musicals. This was just a record place. But I must've said something right during the interview, because they immediately offered me a part-time job.

I started out at the proverbial bottom, doing whatever no one else wanted to do, most of which involved hauling things from one place to another, be it an interoffice memo from the mailroom to the MGM floor, or a box of records from the MGM floor to the Verve floor. Naturally, music always piped out of everyone's office, and during my first months, I'd walk down the hall and be treated to the sounds of the British Invasion, specifically Herman's Hermits and Eric Burdon and the Animals.

It wasn't at all glamorous, but I met *everyone*, most notably and fortuitously, the head of the MGM promotional department, Harold Berkman. Harold, an industry

Herman's Hermits' first tour of America, circa 1968

veteran who was about fifteen years my senior, had an open door policy, and I took advantage, hanging out at his office for hours, listening to him do his hustle with the radio stations and his national staff. "Hey, baby," he'd say in his thick Baltimore accent, "ya gotta get this record on the air. I don't care how you do it, baby. It can come in the front door, or the back door, or the side door. Just make it happen, baby." (With Harold, there was always a lot of "baby.") I'd never met anyone like Harold, and he must've seen something in me, because he stole me out of the mailroom and brought me aboard as his assistant.

Back then, "assistant" didn't mean what it means today. I wasn't parked at a desk, answering phones, keeping schedules, and sending out memos. No, I had my fingers in everything, and I soaked it all in, thrilled that my love of music

Ron Weisner with Harold Berkman, Erroll Garner, and Mike Becce

had dovetailed with my professional life. And Harold was my guide. If he was working on something he thought would help me with my career, he'd explain it. If I had a question, he'd answer it honestly, and at great length. He didn't have to do any of this, but he must've recognized something in me that I didn't even know was there.

In addition to acting as Harold's right (and sometimes left) hand, I also worked closely with the press department—it wasn't the media department, as is the case today, just press—and watched how they'd take one of MGM's British Invasion acts, lock them into a room for a week, and make them do interview after interview after interview. And none of these artists complained. No one played diva. Everyone had one goal: do what needed to be done to get their music on the radio, to get their faces in a magazine, and to get their fans into the store to buy their record. I also went to every promotional party I could, where I'd play fly-on-the-wall and silently listen to the label and radio people do their hustle . . . although few of them did it as well as my man, Harold Berkman.

(Harold was a part of my life for the rest of his life. In 1972, when I moved to California, Harold followed suit, and, out of the music industry at this point, he opened up a car wash. Sadly, the car wash was a disaster and closed almost as quickly as it opened, and he fell into a deep depression. He was incommunicado for a bit, then, when he reemerged, he started a combination messenger service and limo service. A few months later, the fax machine became a common office tool and killed the messenger side of his business, so he shifted his focus to the limos. He utilized his connections in the music world—even though he'd been away from the industry for years, he still had plenty of connections; everyone loved Harold—to land clients. It took off, and his company, Music Express, is now one of the largest, busiest, most prestigious limo services in the world. And here's what kind of guy Harold Berkman was: A goodly number of his hires were former record label employees who'd fallen on hard times. What a *mensch*. I was lucky to know him.)

In 1967, after a year of working under Harold, I was relocated to the Verve floor. Soon after I started in their promotions department, Verve launched a subsidiary label called Verve Forecast. It was quite the alternative to Verve, who was known for their records by jazz greats like Ella Fitzgerald (my idol), Wes Montgomery, Jimmy Smith, Cal Tjader, Stan Getz, Count Basie, Oscar Peterson, and Charlie Parker. Forecast, on the other hand, took a completely different stylistic tack, inking such future rock, folk, and blues icons as Richie Havens, the Velvet Underground, John Lee Hooker, and Dave van Ronk. They also put out Laura Nyro's first album *More Than a New Discovery*, a record that holds a special place in my heart, as I was in the studio when she cut "Stoney End." Janis Ian's self-titled debut was another favorite, especially the track "Society's Child," a song about an interracial romance that was way ahead of its time.

Going from MGM to Verve, then from Verve to Verve Forecast did wonders for my music biz education. All three labels were in the same building, in the same industry, under the same umbrella, but when it came to promoting their artists, all three operated differently, primarily because each label was a different genre, and there wasn't much crossover in terms of radio and print outlets. Also, MGM's company structure was such that someone like me was able to bop from department to department, so I learned everything there was to learn about the industry: marketing, A&R (artist and repertoire, for all you non-industry types), distribution, the works. The more people I met, the more connections I made, and the more connections I made, the more information I gathered. (The vast majority of the folks at the label were flat-out nice, and they were more than happy to show the ropes to a wet-behind-the-ears guy like me. Today, record label jobs are few and far between and are held onto for dear life. I can't blame anyone for that—everyone has bills to pay—but it makes me pine for the days of quality, sincere mentorship.)

I even spent a fair amount of time hanging out with the Verve quality control man, whose job it was to make certain the record pressings were on point. He worked in what was called a cutting room, which was filled with machines galore. Often when I poked my head in, he'd have a giant hunk of vinyl on his table, on which he'd burn the grooves, a process that, to me, was otherworldly. We could always tell when he was pressing the vinyl because the hallway near the cutting room reeked like a steaming car wreck, and when I smelled that smell, if I had the time, I'd go into the room and listen to these hot-off-the-press pressings of, say, the new Wes Montgomery album. It was magic.

Another aspect that made the entire MGM experience special was the sense of working as a team. Everyone pulled in the same direction at the same time. And when some of the folks on your team have a gift—be it the gift of gab, or of preternatural perseverance, or of an encyclopedic knowledge of every word that Billie Holiday ever sang—man, it doesn't get any better.

Being that I made dozens of trips up and down MGM and Verve hallways on a daily basis, I became friendly with pretty much everyone, but I became especially tight with my fellow jacks-of-all-trades, Neil Bogart and Cecil Holmes.

Neil, Cecil, and I gravitated toward one another in part because we were among the younger people in the company, and in part because we were all music nuts. The majority of our bonding took place at live shows, but we didn't bond only with one another; we also made it a point to become friendly with the talent. I think the singers and instrumentalists liked us because we weren't the executives (aka "The Suits"), but rather eager young fans who happened to work at a record label. The Suits—who were, across the board, good people—recognized that we'd established good relationships with the artists, so if they needed an act to, say, spend an entire day doing radio interviews, or do a signing at a record store, they'd ask us to arrange it, then to cart the act around the city.

Neil and Cecil were both from New Jersey, and their level of street smarts was off the charts. Even in his early twenties, Neil was a brilliant promotions and marketing man, at once aggressive and charming. From the time we first met, he talked about starting his own company and bringing Cecil and I into the fold. That appealed to me not because I necessarily wanted to run my own label, but rather because I'd get to spend all day, every day with my fellow psycho music fanatics.

The View from Cecil Holmes

When Ron and I worked at MGM, we spent a lot of time on public transportation, carrying boxes and boxes of records. (As radio promotion guys, we had to take the buses and the trains to all the local stations—and I say had to, because neither of us had a car.) We got some funny looks; here we were, these teenage-looking kids, one black and one white, hauling cargo. I can only imagine what people thought. We did that all the time, and that's how we became friends, and when you're Ron's friend, there's nothing he wouldn't do for you.

I remember one time we had to go up to the Apollo Theater, and I told him, "Wait for me before you go. You'll be better off if I'm with you." I turned around, and he was gone. He went there without me. I was concerned about him, but he'd been there a million times, so I guess he knew what he was doing.

The more Neil talked about starting his own label, the more he convinced me that it wasn't just a pipe dream. (Then again, Neil was such a good pitchman that if he wanted to, he could convince someone to buy a bag of air.) His belief was that we could build a company with an artist-friendly atmosphere unlike any other label out there. We were young, we were energetic, we had our ears to the ground, we could relate to artists of all genres, and we weren't Suits. Plus, if you were in a room with Neil for two minutes, you could tell that he was the kind of person who would kill to make what he wanted to happen, happen.

Neil's goal was to be successful doing things that other companies weren't doing, to do things that no one else even understood. The message we wanted to convey was, *It's okay to cross the street and work with the guys in the smaller office, because you'll get the chance to do something different, new, and exciting. We're the renegades. Come and join our merry band of outlaws.* If I were a musician, I'd sure as hell want to work with us.

Before I knew it, Neil borrowed money from a mobster—at an insanely high interest rate, naturally—thus they all had a piece of the pie. So a mere eighteen months after I was hired for my first job in the music industry, I was a record executive. Who needed college? (When I told Harold Berkman I was leaving, he gave me some sage advice: "Watch your back, and don't get into anything you can't get out of." Those are words I continue to live by.)

While we were organizing our label—which we called Buddah Records—Neil made a separate distribution deal with a label called Kama Sutra Records, who was having great success with the Lovin' Spoonful. The label was run by three guys who were, for a lack of a better word, strange: Artie Ripp, Phil Stenberg, and Hy Mizahri. Artie—who, in 1971, signed Billy Joel to his first record deal—was hilarious, but he was also a lunatic; ADHD wasn't an actual thing in 1967, but if it was, Artie would've had it, times one hundred. Phil was a husky, good-looking man who was wasted pretty much every hour of the day. And Hy was . . . Hy.

We rented office space at 1650 Broadway, a dumpy structure across the street from the legendary Brill Building that housed a number of other record labels and industry heavies, including the unhinged producer Phil Spector. Phil was, as advertised, completely out of his mind, and every day or two, we'd be treated to the sound of a woman screaming, and the sight of said woman being chased to the elevator by a gun-toting Spector. And I sure as hell can understand why those women screamed the way they did. Whenever I was in a confined space with Phil, specifically the elevator, I was scared shitless, especially when he'd go into one of his rants. The guy could rant about anything: the record industry, the weather, his crappy deli sandwich. He was loud and barely coherent, with a palpable sense of nuttiness that put those street corner preachers in Times Square to shame. Over time, Phil became less scary and more amusing. I wish I could've recorded some of those elevator rants. They were priceless.

(From the ridiculous to the sublime, on the other side of the hall sat the office of a music publisher by the name of Tony Orlando. And yes, we're talking the same Tony Orlando who had a massive hit with "Tie a Yellow Ribbon." The Isley Brothers were on the next floor up, and they'd covered the walls of their offices with floor-to-ceiling mirrors. And the smell in there . . . *whoa*. You could probably get a contact high all the way in the lobby.)

We hired a couple of secretaries, turned on the phones, and got to work, and we worked *hard*. We knew that we didn't have the money or power of the MGMs of the world, so if we were going to survive and thrive, we'd have to out-hustle and outthink them. But before we could do anything, we had to sign some artists who could move some records.

The beginning: Joe Fields, Neil Bogart, Ron Weisner, Jack Hakim, and Cecil Holmes.
Buddah Records 1969.

Our first major signing—and I give full credit to Neil—
was a songwriting/production duo called Super K Productions. Jerry Kasenetz and Jeff Katz had a great feel for
bubblegum pop—and considering the simplicity of the
music, that isn't as simple as you might think. Jerry and
Jeffrey delivered us a bunch of music from three of their
many studio projects: the Ohio Express, the 1910 Fruitgum
Company, and the Kasenetz-Katz Singing Orchestra Circus. It was disposable music, cheap to record and easy for
listeners to digest, and even though it didn't do much for
our credibility in the music world, it was exactly what we

needed business-wise. Their early albums and singles sold quite well and eventually earned us a shitload of money, so much so that we were able to afford to sign acts whose music we actually cared about, like The Impressions and The Isley Brothers.

Kasenetz and Katz's bubblegum acts didn't always get on the radio of their own accord. This was the heyday of payola, which is a civil way of saying we bribed the shit out of radio. The best deejays in the biggest cities had carte blanche to pick their own music, unlike today, when the station's program director is in charge. Songs were often divided up into two groups, the day parts and the night parts, which, as you might guess, was the way of delineating which tunes were to be played when it was light outside and which when it was dark. Some music was played all day and night, but those slots were filled by the likes of the Beatles . . . that is, unless you or someone from your label slipped the deejay something. And that something could be clothes, plane tickets, or, as was mostly the case, cash. Sometimes it would cost a sawbuck, sometimes a hundred, and sometimes a thousand. It wasn't exactly kosher, but we did what had to be done.

More so than the rest of the Buddah team, Neil traveled around the country, in hopes of finding the Next Big Thing—and because he had golden ears, more often than not, he did. For example, once in the summer of 1969, he called me from a radio station in San Francisco, yelling so loudly that if I opened the window, I probably could've heard him in Midtown. *"Ronnie, I'm listening to this record right now, and it's the number one most requested song in the city, and it defies genre. It's got some rock, and some R&B, and some soul, but if you had to call it one thing, you'd call it gospel, and I'm gonna track the guy down and buy the rights!"*

After I got my hearing back, I said, "Sounds great, Neil." And it did. He was an enthusiastic music fan, but he never got *that* excited without good reason. "Who's the group?"

"The Edwin Hawkins Singers. The song's called 'Oh, Happy Day.'"

In typical Buddah fashion, we moved fast—two weeks later, it was in stores, and two weeks after that, it hit the top ten. Not too long thereafter, Edwin's album went gold, and it won the Grammy for Best Gospel Record. If I'd have heard the song, I'd have thought, "That's a great record," and that's it. When Neil heard the record, he thought, "*Smash*," and that's why Neil was Neil. He understood that this song transcended genre, that it was a message of hope and positivity that would resonate beyond a core gospel audience and attract anyone with a heart. And he was 100 percent right. That summer, you couldn't listen to the radio for an hour without hearing that song.

Edwin, who's the nicest guy you'll ever meet, was far removed from the record industry, and his naïveté and enthusiasm were at once charming and disarming. When we were preparing for his tour, he told me, "Ronnie, I want to take the entire choir with me."

"That's great, Edwin. How many people are in the choir?"

"Sixty-three."

"Edwin."

"What?"

"You can't."

He looked brokenhearted. "Why not?

"You just . . . you just . . . you just *can't*. You can't take sixty-three people on the road."

"But I have to. It's the church. It's my family."

"Edwin, the cost of transporting so many people would be, um, prohibitive. You'd need five tour buses. *Nobody* uses five tour buses. And the hotel bills alone. . . ."

"All right. I understand. Let me think on it."

A few days later, he called: "I cut down the number. It won't be a problem now."

"That's great, Edwin," I said. "How many?"

"Forty-three."

I sighed. "Edwin, that's still a whole lot of bodies." I then gave him some specific cost figures.

"Wow," he said. The next week, the headcount was down to sixteen, and that number worked for everyone, so they took to the road, played some great shows, and sold more records.

Like every A&R person in history, Neil's ears and heart sometimes led him astray, the most notable instance being a sloppy rock band called Elephant's Memory. Best known for their early-1970s work with John Lennon, Elephant's Memory formed in 1967 and soon made a name for themselves in Greenwich Village. How and why they managed to make a name for themselves was beyond me, because they were terrible, a true train wreck of a group. Neil, for reasons he never explained, and for reasons I still can't figure out, was obsessed with them. "These guys are gonna break big," he told me and Cecil during one of our daily wrap-up meetings, "and I'm gonna spend as much as I need to make that happen, and we're gonna do this huge showcase, and everybody's gonna be there, and we're gonna make an amazing album with them, and. . . ." Neil went on in that vein for about ten minutes, never once stopping to take a breath. He was Evelyn Wood speed-talking.

After he finally ran out of gas, I said, "Neil, those idiots are horrible, but I'm with you. I'll go down with the ship."

I knew that Elephant's Memory had no chance of succeeding beyond their core fan base of Lower East Side drug heads, because they themselves were Lower East Side drug heads who had the uncanny ability to fuck up every good opportunity. Plus you couldn't have a rational conversation with any of them; it was as if you were speaking English, and they were speaking Martian. Plus, as noted, they were terrible. But we didn't bother arguing with Neil, because once that man got an idea in his head, nothing was going to keep him from seeing it through until the bitter end.

The next week, I went to their rehearsal space to determine if they were ready for the showcase. The first thing I noticed when I walked in were the enormous inflatable animals strewn throughout the room. For the next forty-five minutes, I listened to them be terrible, all while standing next to a six-foot-tall blow-up monkey. On the subway back to the office, I thought, *Maybe it's me. Maybe Neil's right. Maybe I'm just missing it.*

But I wasn't.

All the right people came to the showcase—the right writers, the right television personalities, the right tastemakers, the right musicians—and the scene was set for a massive success. The only problem was—surprise, surprise—the band was awful. It was an embarrassing, expensive nightmare for which I spent a lot of time apologizing. My press friends gave me shit about that show for years, and whenever they did, I just had to sit there and take it.

This sort of stuff didn't happen to us often, but when it did, it pissed off the Buddah numbers guy, Art Kass, to no end. Art wanted to keep us afloat, while Neil was willing to spend $50 to earn back $20, just to prove his point. But even Neil couldn't spend enough on Elephant's Memory to make them sound like professional musicians. That said, they weren't a complete failure: The producers of the film *Midnight Cowboy* used two of the band's songs on the soundtrack. They clearly knew something Cecil and I didn't, because that album *Songs from Midnight Cowboy* moved a few copies. It wasn't a hit, and it didn't make back Neil's investment in the band, but he nonetheless considered it a triumph. Cecil, Art, and I considered it a fiasco. Eventually Neil agreed, probably around the time that all the bills started coming in.

The View from Cecil Holmes

One time, Ron and I went to a big music convention in upstate New York. The artists and the record label people were staying on the same grounds, but in different buildings. Our building wasn't an A-plus accommodation, if you know what I mean, but the main house where the stars were staying, well, that was nice. Ron and I decided we wanted some of that action, so we walked up the hill to the main building to see what we could do.

We marched right on over to the reception desk, and Ron said to the guy, "I think we have a reservation."

"Are you sure?" he said, "Because these rooms are all booked for the artists who are part of the convention."

Ron said, "We are artists."

I whispered, "We are?" He shushed me.

"Who are you?" asked the clerk.

"The Smothers Brothers."

"Let me go check," he said, then walked back to get the reservation book.

I said, "Ronnie, what're you doing, man? They're gonna figure out we ain't brothers."

But apparently they didn't. For one night, we had the A-plus room. And if Tom and Dick Smothers ended up in the coach house, I apologize.

Because things were going so well with Kama Sutra, we got deeper into distribution, picking up a handful of regional labels, including Sussex Records, which was out in LA, and Hot Wax, right out of Detroit. (I even got into the act, tracking down a rock group out of Pittsburgh called the Jaggerz, who had a local hit with "The Rapper." I brought the record back to New York, Neil approved, and they broke nationally.) This wasn't a normal business model, but nothing about Buddah was normal. We were the crazy guys, always working the angles, always hustling, but our madness paid off in the form of consistent radio play. Now that doesn't sound like a major coup, but back then, radio was *everything*. If your record was on the airwaves, your record sold, and it sold well. And the Sussexes and the Hot Waxes of the world didn't have the staff, the means, or the time to work the streets like we did, so for a small piece of their pie, we'd steer their promotional and distribution ship, and thus break their artists. Never once did anyone from any of these labels complain about how much they were paying us; they realized that it was far more advantageous to have a part of *something* than all of *nothing.*

Arguably our most fulfilling regional distribution deal was with Curtom Records, a Chicago label overseen by The Impressions lead singer, Curtis Mayfield, and the band's manager, Eddie Thomas. They brought us what I consider to be some of the finest music we ever distributed, especially The Impressions albums *This Is My Country* and *The Young Mods' Forgotten Story,* all five of the albums from the Five Stairsteps of "O-o-h Child" fame, and Curtis's own brilliant *Super Fly.* (Side note: Many listeners and critics seemed shocked when Curtis released *Super Fly,* saying it was a sharp left turn from the music of The Impressions, but the fact of the matter is that Curtis had been trending in that funkier direction throughout the second half of the 1960s. If people had paid closer attention, they wouldn't have been at all taken aback. The point I'm making is that The Impressions gave the world considerably more brilliant music than "People Get Ready" and "Keep on Pushin'.") All three members of The Impressions—Curtis, Fred Cash, and Sam Gooden—were as classy as it got. They were a pleasure to be around, and Curtis must've liked something I was doing, because I worked with him after Buddah closed its doors. (More about that later.)

The majority of the material we released from these small labels were singles—not too many of these bands had much to offer beyond their one great song—and if you look at it casually, that may not seem like enough for a company to hang its hat on. But when you take it as a whole, all of a sudden, we had an honest-to-goodness catalog that signaled to artists and labels that Buddah was a place to go if you wanted a hit. Sure, you might receive a bigger advance or better distribution from MGM, or Liberty, or Columbia, or RCA, but you wouldn't have a bunch of nuts like Neil, Cecil, and me—guys who knew how and where to spread the money, guys who knew where all the bodies were buried— pounding the pavement for you.

An inordinate number of our artists were making regular television appearances, so I was commuting from New York to Los Angeles on a near-weekly basis to make sure our acts' regular appearances on *Midnight Special* or *Rock Concert* or *The Tonight Show* went smoothly. After a year and a half of back and forth and back and forth, I was exhausted, so I suggested to Neil that we open a West Coast office. Being that a West Coast office would've consisted of me, an assistant, and a gopher hanging out in a small, two-floor building on Sunset and Doheny, Neil agreed.

After a year of status quo, several artists asked me if I'd be interested in managing them. I never had any designs on running anyone's career, but I'd become quite close with several members of our roster and had a vested emotional interest in their success and happiness, so I officially took on my first clients—Gladys Knight, Sha Na Na, and Wonder Woman herself, Lynda Carter—while I was still working for the label. Wearing two hats became quite hectic, so the question became, did I want to leave Buddah and devote my professional life to managing? Fortunately, that was answered for me. In 1973, Neil and Cecil decided they wanted to move to LA and start another label, which was eventually called Casablanca Records.* I took that as a sign that it was time to get out of the record business and into the people business.

The music world is full of horror stories about coke-sniffing record label executives and LSD-soaked musicians, but none of that applied at Buddah. (I, myself, rarely partook in drugs. After seeing the havoc they could wreak, they scared the shit out of me.) Our employees and artists were, across the board, classy, quality people, professional and driven. We didn't have any divas in the office, in the studio, or on the stage. We had no assholes, just people who were committed to what they were doing, be it making the music, marketing the music, or selling the music. I think that stemmed from the precept that if you committed to us, then we committed to you, and that sort of collaborative attitude wouldn't be attractive to a diva type, to someone who has little interest in being part of a team.

Me, I love teams. And I sure as hell loved Buddah.

....

* Considering Neil's uncanny ability to hit on an idea that'll make money, Casablanca was wildly successful. During his reign, the roster ran the gamut from Kiss, to Parliament-Funkadelic, to Donna Summer, but they were best-known for riding the disco wave. Neil passed away in 1982 and remained a friend until the end.

CHAPTER TWO

Sports

*Music was number one, two, and three in my heart,
but if there was a number four, it was boxing. And
for boxing, number one was Muhammad Ali.*

Neil, Cecil, Art, and I were generally the only attendees at Buddah's end-of-the-day meeting. When we had special guest stars, it almost always meant something big was brewing. Or if not big, at least interesting.

The special guest stars on the 1969 summer afternoon in question were a stuffy-looking lawyer and a not-stuffy-looking composer named Oscar Brown Jr.* After introductions were made, I said, "Fill me in."

Neil explained, "Oscar here wrote the songs for a musical, and they're looking for investors so they can get it to off-Broadway. They also need somebody to do the original cast album." An original cast album is, in effect, a soundtrack for a play.

Buddah had never invested in a play, nor had we ever done an original cast album, but that was the fun of being

....

* Coincidentally, in the late '90s, Brown, also a vocalist and songwriter, cut a couple of records for the third (or maybe fourth) incarnation of Verve Records.

there: Something new (or interesting, or weird) was always around the corner. I said, "What kind of play?"

"It's called *Big Time Buck White*," Neil said. "Oscar, would you care to fill us in?"

Oscar went ahead and filled us in, but his synopsis was rambling and didn't make much sense. When he came to a stop, I asked, "Who's in the play?"

The lawyer grinned and said, "Muhammad Ali."

"You're kidding," I said.

"I'm not," the lawyer replied. "He's signed. He's committed. He's ready." I knew Ali had a lot of free time; his boxing license had been suspended two years before as punishment for his refusal to fulfill his military duty and fight in Vietnam. "Are you guys interested?" the lawyer asked.

I raised my hand like a schoolkid. "I am! And I'll be the point person!" In some ways, this was a typical Buddah endeavor, in that we were the only nutcases nutty enough to put money into a theater production anchored by a noted thespian such as Muhammad Ali. But nothing will stick to the wall unless you throw it, so we threw, and off we went. Soon, the papers were drawn up and signed, and I was Muhammad Ali's official Buddah Records handler.

Two days later, I went to a rehearsal space on the west side of Manhattan. I opened up the door, poked my nose in, and there were about twenty people surrounding a tall figure: Ali. As soon as the actors stopped running lines, the lawyer waved me over and introduced me to the man himself. Ali had an aura about him, happy-go-lucky, always looking to get a laugh. (I found out later that one of his favorite jokes was to sneak up behind you and flick you in the earlobe. Then, when you turned around, he'd be five feet away, staring up into space with an innocent look plastered on his mug. That's how damn fast his hands and legs were. He also liked doing tacky magic tricks, the less about which are said, the better. Suffice it to say that when he did one for you, you'd better laugh.)

Over the next few months, Ali and I spent a lot of time together, and he turned out to be a great, great guy. He was still in his physical prime, handsome and cut, and had a stature about him that was unlike anything I'd ever been around. He was a people person and went out of his way to make sure that everyone was entertained. Way more fun than Elephant's Memory.

As for the play, I went to a number of the rehearsals, and, well, it wasn't so hot. I wasn't concerned, though, figuring these people were professionals—Ali being the lone exception—and it would come together over time. But I wasn't a theater connoisseur, and there was the distinct possibility I wouldn't even be able to tell if it came together, so I kept my mouth shut. This wasn't like a record, where I could help out with the creative aspect of things. My job here wasn't quality control. My job was to get things done.

Besides, I didn't give a shit.

See, that play could've been the worst piece of shit in the history of theater, or it could've been a brilliant production of Shakespeare's long-lost comedy, but it didn't make a damn bit of difference to me. The only thing I cared about was the fact that I got to hang out with the Greatest of All Time, the Champ, the former Cassius Clay.

It turned out that *Big Time Buck White* wasn't the worst piece of shit in the history of theater. It was, according to the vast majority of the newspaper critics, *one of* the worst pieces of shit in the history of theater, and it closed in under a week. But I always wondered if it was really that bad, or if the newspaper writers were using their platform to help bring down a man who was taking a right and just stand against his government.

The play disappeared, along with Buddah's investment, which was in the neighborhood of $200,000, but that didn't stop us from diving back into the sports ocean.

Later that year, the New York Mets, after almost a decade of embarrassing futility, managed to win the World Series. In a decision that set music back about six decades, we released an album of songs warbled by the Champs called *The Amazing Mets*. The entire album was recorded in one night, but I don't think it would've mattered if we'd have spent one year in the studio—no amount of time was going to make Tom Seaver or Jerry Koosman sound good. In what was probably a world's record, the album was in New York stores only two days after it was recorded. The local media were in a Mets frenzy, and every scrap of information relating to the team was treated as a major news story, so *The Amazing Mets* became our buzziest record to date. Did it make back the money we lost from the Ali play? Not quite. Was it the greatest piece of music in history? Not even close. Would I invest in a Muhammad Ali play today? God, yes.* Was I proud to be a part of a company that would do something as daring and ridiculous as *The Amazing Mets?*

Hell yes.

....

* Whenever I run into Ali, I tell him, "Champ, the best money I ever lost was on you." That always elicits a hug from him.

CHAPTER THREE

Knight

We've shared the ups. We've shared the downs. We've shared it all.

What with the conspicuous success of the Impressions, Curtis Mayfield, the Five Stairsteps, and Bill Withers, Buddah Records's reputation in the R&B world was impeccable. So when Gladys Knight and the Pips's contract with Motown Records ran out, and Gladys wasn't happy with how she was treated, we thought Buddah would be the perfect landing place for her and the Pips.

And man, did we want her; the thing is, we had no clue how to get her. We didn't have the major labels' means. We couldn't give her hundreds of thousands of dollars of tour support. We couldn't plaster billboards all up and down Sunset Boulevard. We couldn't have a record release party at Madison Square Garden. However, we had one thing that nobody else had: *us*. Nobody had our energy, or drive, or balls. We would kill for her, which is something that Motown never did for her in the past, and something that no other label would do for her in the future. We normally did the work of ten men each; for her, we'd do that of twenty.

Don't get me wrong: Motown was phenomenal. They opened up doors and broke down walls, but come the late 1960s, they seemed to be more interested in perpetuating the Motown brand rather than developing their acts. They'd become a corporation—a small corporation, but a corporation nonetheless—and we were a bunch of crazy guys who were going to eat, sleep, and breathe Gladys Knight and the Pips.

We had numerous meetings with Gladys, who was accompanied by her brother Bubba Knight and her cousins William Guest and Eddie Patten, aka the Pips. We must've said or done something right, because not only did we not scare them off but also they signed a deal with us for a substantially lower advance than they could've gotten elsewhere.

Once the papers were signed, I was thrilled—hell, I was *beyond* thrilled. I thought, *Now I've made it.* Don't get me wrong: Curtis Mayfield and Bill Withers weren't anything to sneeze at, but this was *Gladys Knight!* "Every Beat of My Heart"! "Letter Full of Tears"! And she was *ours!* All of a sudden, I was the little fourteen-year-old pisher sitting in the balcony at the Apollo, freaking out over my favorite singer. And to top it all off, Gladys and the guys were *cool,* great people who were really into their music, who hugged you when you walked into the room, who, when they asked "How are you," sincerely wanted to know. Each and every day during the week after we finalized the deal, I listened to my Gladys Knight cassette tapes on the long drive to and from work, thinking some version of, *Man, look at what I'm doing. Look who I'm working with. I am one lucky son of a bitch. There's nothing better.*

Buddah didn't have house producers and writers like the Motowns and the Philly Souls of the world, but that gave us the freedom to match our artist with the perfect collaborator, and, in this case, we decided on Tony Camillo. Tony was one of the most sought-after composer/arranger/producers of the era, and he had shared the studio with Stevie Wonder, the Supremes, and Parliament, among many others. Gladys wasn't a prolific composer, and she had no problem working with other artists, as long as she was comfortable with them and their attitude, and Tony passed all of her tests.

Backtracking to 1968, when Neil, Cecil, and I were at MGM, Verve had an act called Gordian Knot. They didn't sell much, nor did they garner much press, but the three of us liked the band and always kept tabs on them, specifically their leader, Jim Weatherly. Jim was a hell of a writer and contributed five songs to Gladys's Buddah debut *Imagination,* including Gladys's biggest hit—and, to some, one of the greatest pop songs of all time—"Midnight Train to Georgia."

When I heard the early mix of the album, my first thought was, *This is going to be the biggest record of my life.* My second thought: *Christ, we got lucky.* My third thought: *I'm so happy for Gladys.* My fourth thought: *We've gotta do right by them.*

And that fourth thought was the most important. During those initial meetings, Neil, Cecil, and I went on and on about how we were going to do everything in our power to break her record, and when we did everything in our power, nobody could touch us. Fortunately, we delivered, and then some.

It all started with radio, which, at that time, was just about the only way to break an R&B song. If you weren't on top of your game and didn't keep the deejays and program directors on your side, you weren't going to have a hit, period, even with a song as brilliant as "Midnight Train to Georgia." You might have one or two good weeks, but unless you schmoozed the right person, or greased the proper palm, you were done.

Suffice it to say that we took care of business. But we wanted more. We wanted to cross over.

If a project was only serviced to black radio and print, it had a sales ceiling, no matter if you were Gladys Knight, Bobby Knight, Knight Rider, or a knight in shining armor. But if you could get white radio to play it, then you could get white America to buy it. This may seem obvious, but back then, it wasn't. It was far from the norm, but Buddah didn't give a shit. We were the renegades, and our attitude was, *Let the people decide what they want to hear, not some asshole who thinks that R&B won't work on his station because they don't have enough black listeners.*

The single received plenty of airplay and sold plenty of copies, plus Gladys and the Pips put on a brilliant live show, and they loved touring, so when they took to the road, great concerts led to positive word of mouth, and positive word of mouth led to a jump in sales, and a jump in sales led to more radio airplay, and more radio airplay led to another jump in sales, all of which led to the top spot on the *Billboard* Hot 100, and her second Grammy award.

In 1973, Barbra Streisand had a massive hit with "The Way We Were," and as it climbed up the charts, Gladys began performing it during her live shows. It sounded so spectacular, and the crowd's reaction was so positive, that I told her, "Gladys, you have to record this."

Gladys was (and is) as modest a person as you'll ever meet, so it was no surprise when she told me, "No. Absolutely not. How could I even consider that? It's Barbra's song."

I put my hand on her shoulder and said, "Gladys, this is yours now. This is your song. You own it. Or at least co-own it."

"I don't know, Ronnie," she said.

We went back and forth on it for days, until finally she was convinced. We put it on the album *I Feel a Song*, and after we released the single, it shot up to number eleven on the *Billboard* chart. It's still in her repertoire to this day, and if you see her perform it and you don't get chills, you need to get your ears checked.

Gladys was (and is) beloved in the industry, and seemingly everyone wanted to share a bill with her, which led to some fortuitous encounters. She and Sammy Davis Jr. played a bunch of Vegas shows together, and during that time, I grew close to Sammy, his wife, Altovise, and his attorney, Sonny Murray. It turned out that Sammy had some tax troubles, so when he died in 1990, the IRS impounded all of his belongings: the house, the cars, the storage lockers, *everything.* Sonny brought me in for a meeting, in hopes that I could come up with an idea that could help Altovise keep enough money to live a normal life. I asked Sonny what was in the lockers; he ran through the list, the last item of which was dozens of master tapes from both studio sessions and live gigs.

Gladys Knight, American Cancer Society tribute

"The IRS wants money. What're they gonna do with master tapes?" I asked. Neither of them had an answer. I continued: "I don't know the specifics of your situation, and don't know how bad it is, but here's a suggestion: Contact the IRS and tell them to give back the tapes, then I'll put together a deal with a label—I don't know who yet, but somebody'll bite—then we'll release a box set, and half of everything could go to the IRS, and half can go to Altovise, and everybody will be happy."

Miracle of miracles, the IRS agreed. On one hand, that was terrific, because Altovise could have her house back, but on the other, it was a mess, because yours truly had to figure out how to make magic from Sammy's tapes. It took weeks of listening and researching, but eventually I figured out what was what and when was when, and next thing you know, we had ourselves a nice little package that sold more than a few copies. None of that would have happened if Gladys and I weren't a team.

I've been through so much with Gladys. I've known her for forty years. We've seen some amazing times together—top ten hits, awards, sold-out shows—and some horrific times, including the sudden and premature death of her son James. She knows I'll always be there for her, and I know she'll always be there for me. Who'd have thought when we stole her away from Motown, I was getting not only a brilliant artist but also a best friend.

The View from Gladys Knight

My group had been with Motown Records for a little bit more than seven years, and our contract was up. To tell the honest truth, there were a lot of good things that happened at Motown, and I mention that because I've talked a lot about the down side of the label, but they opened a lot of doors for me and many black artists. Actually, the reason we went there in the first place is because they opened so many doors. Our mentors were Maurice King and Cholly Atkins, and they always told us, "You don't want to be the kind of act who has just one hit record. You want to be around for a long time." So we wanted to stay with them . . . except Motown had issues with money. Let's just say they had a problem with the royalty thing.

Ultimately, we just wanted a label who believed in us, because in the record business, that's the only way you're going to get the support you need to do what you need to do. Look at Berry Gordy and Diana Ross. Berry is why Diana got so huge, because you heard nothing but her name coming from his mouth. I don't care who else was on that label, but all Berry talked about was how great Diana was. We wanted a company who felt that way about us, a company who didn't schmooze us, a company who believed in us and what we were trying to do.

The first thing that grabbed me about Ron was how much he loved music. Like me, he always wanted to make it as good as he could make it. We immediately became friends because our spirits are alike, and that's why we went with Buddah. See, I base my decisions on people, and Ron's a real guy. I can tell when somebody's stroking me, and I can tell when somebody cares. Ron, Neil Bogart, Cecil Holmes, and Art Kass all had that glint in their eye, the glint of real people.

Everybody, but everybody told us, "Y'all got to be crazy to go with Buddah. They ain't got no money, they ain't got no staff, they don't know how to make hits. What are y'all thinking?" But we felt like that was the company we needed to be with, and we made the right decision. After watching Ron, Neil, and Cecil bend over backwards for us, I knew we had a family.

When I got ready to leave the Pips, I needed someone to lean on, and Ron was the first guy I thought of. When I asked him to be my manager, he said, "I'll do what I can." He didn't talk a big game like some managers do. This isn't to take anything away from my previous managers, but they were accountants first and managers second. Ron's a music guy, and the way he works, well, let's just say he's soooo helpful.

He was in to who you were, and how you could best do what you do, not how much money you could make for him, or he could make for you.

You may not hear Ron's name—which is what he wants—but he's done some awesome things for the record industry, and you don't find people like him. Today, we're just friends. He's no longer my manager . . . but I wish he were. I'm glad that God put me and Ron on this earth at the same time, so he could be my mentor, my friend, and my brother.

CHAPTER FOUR

Mayfield

Curtis Mayfield was a poet the way that Bob Dylan was a poet.

If you're the creative force behind a band—the lead singer, the composer, the arranger—at some point, you'll probably want to flex your muscles on your own. It's doesn't mean you disrespect the people you've been working with, and it's probably not about ego. You just have something to say, and you want to say it by yourself. That might upset fans of the group, but all true artists change and grow, and they want their listeners to change and grow with them.

To me, Curtis Mayfield was one of the great storytellers and wordsmiths of our era, as borne out by the fact that his lyrics have more than withstood the test of time and are as relevant, if not *more* relevant, than they were twenty, thirty, and forty years ago. While I never pushed him to leave The Impressions, I was more than a little curious to find out what he'd do after he struck out on his own. His first two solo albums—1970's *Curtis* and 1971's *Roots*—were the next logical step from what The Impressions had been doing for the latter part of the 1960s. But he must've been thinking about moving into another direction, because in 1972, when a couple of producers named Sig Shore and Hannah Weinstein asked him if he'd like to be involved in scoring a film called *Super Fly*, he seemed ready to experiment, to evolve, to move forward.*

Little did we know just how ready he was. Little did we know that he was poised to take a gigantic artistic step forward. Little did we know that he would go on to make what I, and many others, still consider to be the greatest soundtrack album of all time, bar none.

Part of the reason this was such a perfect marriage of movie and musician was that Curtis understood the film. *Super Fly* is labeled a blaxploitation film, and while that is a fair label, it was early enough in the blaxploitation movement that the movie was more than a simple way to make a quick buck. It was shot well, the acting was competent, the plot more than an excuse for chases or fights. But for some reason, Curtis—a man who had created a good life for himself—understood where the film's coke dealers and drug addicts were coming from. He rarely, if ever, crossed paths with that sort of person, but he was such an empathetic man that he could get into their soul, and, by doing so, he created a work of art that elevated the film and captured the ears of millions of listeners who wouldn't have considered paying a dime to see a blaxploitation movie.

All that said, when it was in the theater, it didn't make nearly as much money as did the soundtrack, because while the movie was good, the soundtrack was genius. I was more

---

* When Curtis left The Impressions, there was zero acrimony. Until the day he died, Curtis loved Fred and Sam, and they loved him back. Considering the content of their songs, are you surprised?

than a little proud to have played a small role in the album, because this was a record that touched people, that affected people, that effected change. It was everywhere, and I was in the middle of it. And Curtis Mayfield—this genius, this poet, this gentle soul—was my *friend*. Sometimes I just sat in my office, listened to, say, "Pusherman" or "No Thing on Me," and thought, *Holy shit, I'm a lucky guy.*

"Freddie's Dead" was nominated for the Grammy Award for Best Male R&B Vocal Performances, and we felt Curtis should perform on the show. The Grammy producers disagreed, believing that because the movie and many of the song's lyrics were about drugs, it would send a bad message. (That was absurd. This was 1972, remember, and the country was a mess; there were far worse messages being sent than "Freddie's Dead.") But we convinced them Curtis should sing—how we convinced them shall remain a secret—so the two of us headed down to Nashville.*

The show aired from the Municipal Theater, a fetid, dilapidated shithole, which was one of the reasons Nashville never again hosted the Grammys. The show's director, Walter Miller, concocted a plan for Curtis's performance: have Curtis stand out of sight near the back of the stage, fill the stage with smoke, then have a steadicam fly through the smoke and find Curtis, then follow him until he got to stage center, all the time with the band playing and the lights flashing. It didn't really capture the spirit of the music, but it sounded entertaining, so our team gave it the thumbs-up.

The rehearsal went without a hitch, but in the interest of keeping things moving along, Walter told the stage crew

---

* This was the first and only year the Grammys originated from Music City.

not to go all-out with the smoke. Come show time, during the commercial break before Curtis's performance, they dialed up the smoke machine to full blast, and by the time the commercial ended, you couldn't see shit. After Curtis was introduced and the song kicked off, the steadicam operator took a deep breath, then completely disappeared into the white cloud. "Freddie's Dead" was cranking, and the lights were flashing, and the band was nowhere to be seen. It turned out the blowers that were supposed to get rid of the smoke malfunctioned, plus, as is the case during many live broadcasts, the air conditioner was turned off, thus the air was stagnant, so unless you were standing backstage like me, you didn't see the first three-quarters of the performance. Adding insult to injury, Curtis lost to Billy Paul. "Me and Mrs. Jones" is a perfectly good song, but it's sure as hell no "Freddie's Dead."

At the after-party, I was in a shitty mood, because my friend didn't win an award he absolutely deserved, his performance was marred by a massive technical fuck-up, and I'd just spent five hours in a theater that smelled like the men's restroom at Yankees Stadium. Curtis, on the other hand, was his usual jovial self and was consoling *me* about *his* loss. Near the end of the evening, after I'd gotten a few drinks in me, I told him, "Do me a favor: Get pissed off at *something*, just one time." He just chuckled.

Okay, that's somewhat of an exaggeration. Curtis did get angry once in a while, and when he did, it was inevitably about racism. This I understood, as it was a topic that fascinated and angered me to no end.

My most successful artists were black, and I never felt any sense of racism from them; for that matter, I made lifelong friendships, and these relationships were honest to the point that they confided in me in a manner that was often discomfiting but always enthralling. Late one night, on a tour bus in the middle of England, Curtis and I fell into a discussion about the impact of his lyrics from what I called his Civil Rights Era, songs like "Keep on Pushin'" and "We're a Winner," songs that were the voice of a movement. "Racism is about ignorance," he said. "Most people grow up taught to hate. They don't even know why they're supposed to hate. They're just told that that's what's done. It's inbred."

He then went on to tell me that when he was with The Impressions, the band toured nonstop on buses, and those tours were *tough*. We're talking two shows a night, six days a week, traveling from city to city in an ancient bus. (Can you imagine Justin Timberlake putting up with that kind of schedule? The guy works two days on, then takes five or six off.) When they'd tour the South, they played clubs that were owned and/or run by unabashed racists. More often than you could imagine, when the shows were done, Curtis would track down the owner and ask for their pay, at which point the owner would pull out a gun, call Curtis names I can't bring myself to say, then tell him, "Get out of here, or I'll blow your fucking head off." The Impressions would get on their bus empty-handed and drive off to the next city, hoping against hope that it didn't happen again.

When I was growing up in Brooklyn, I never imagined things like that happened, because we all lived together, and when I say "we all," I mean black, white, Puerto Rican, and all the islanders, and the Russian Jews. We happily coexisted in our apartment building, and when a family had a problem, everyone helped out. A few years later, when we moved to a theoretically better neighborhood in Queens, I started hearing and seeing things that I didn't hear and see in Brooklyn—racial epithets, random violence, out-and-out hatred—and it was all new and horrifying.

So I knew that in terms of race relations, things were bad, but when Curtis told me story after story of mistreatment, well, those talks changed my life. On the other side of the spectrum, you have Joe Jackson, a black guy who was the most racist man I met in my life. (More about him in a bit.)

A quick but pertinent digression: Most of the African-American artists on a record label's roster are assigned to the black music division. That may seem like a logical move, but the audience for a group like, say, the Jacksons was multiracial, and if the promotions people working the project were only reaching out to black radio and retail, and if what little money was spent advertising with black periodicals like *Jet* and *Ebony*, and nothing else, there's a huge chunk of the group's fan base who won't hear or see the record. There was a twisted logic behind this approach. During the 1970s, if a black artist's album was a hit, the sales would max out around 1.3 million, so if a label knew that no matter how much they spent, they'd only be able to sell a finite number of records, what incentive did they have to go above and beyond? Not much, and that's completely understandable. But that didn't mean I had to like it. Or agree with it. Or settle for it. Because it was unacceptable for a single one of my artists to have a ceiling. So I fought it. I'd tell the suits, "We know what our base is. We're making music for the masses. We're making music for *everybody*, so you need to make certain that *everybody* is aware of this album." I had this conversation with dozens of record label employees around 1.3 million times.

But I digress.

After I left Buddah, and after Curtis moved on from Curtom, we still worked together. I wasn't officially his manager, although I performed some managerial duties, but mostly, we were friends. We spoke three or four times a week, and I advised him when I could, although he was whip-smart and didn't need much in the way of advice. Everyone in the industry knew that if you wanted to get to Curtis, I was the guy to call.

In 1990, in the middle of a rinky-dink outdoor show in Harlem, a stage light fell on Curtis, and the blow paralyzed him from the neck down, effectively ending his career. After the accident, I made it a point to get down to his home in Roswell, Georgia, just outside of Atlanta, and spend a couple days with him whenever I could swing it, because he needed time with me, and I needed time with him. We couldn't cut the cord.

We'd talk until he ran out of gas, then we'd pick it up again when he recovered, and because it was Curtis, these talks were deep, meaningful, and honest. One afternoon, I broached the topic of his accident, something I suspected that few others had. "I don't know how you're dealing with this," I told him. "I can't tell you how horrific it makes me feel to see you this way. I'm not trying to depress you, or bring you down, but I've known you for a long time, and you're my dear friend, and this kills me. It really, really kills me. But you have an amazing mind, and an amazing gift, and you can't just shut it down. Curtis, you should start writing again. I can tell just by looking into your eyes that all of that is still there."

Curtis was silent for a bit, then, after clearing his throat, he whispered, "Ronnie, I used to pick up my guitar, and after one strum, the songs would just come out. And that's not gonna happen ever again."

He hated to be seen this way. While he didn't become a recluse, he limited his visitors and *never* did interviews. So when Anthony DeCurtis from *Rolling Stone* called me in 1991 and asked if Curtis would be willing to talk, I gave him an unequivocal no. He called again, and again, I refused. After two more calls and two more refusals, Anthony's boss, Jann Wenner, rang me up. "Ronnie," he said, "you've *got* to let us do this Mayfield interview. It's *really* important. We want to talk to him about his legacy and his impact on today's generation of rappers and singers."

Wenner was a good salesman, so I told him I'd discuss it with Curtis. I immediately called Curtis, explained how hard Wenner was pushing, then said, "Listen, it's entirely up to you."

He paused, then said, "If you think I should do the interview, then I'll do the interview." That was Curtis. Always a pleaser. "Do you think I should?"

I did. Because they were going to be discussing how his music and lyrics affected an entire generation of musicians, rather than his physical state, I thought it was important, because Curtis deserved to be celebrated. Plus I felt that a salutatory feature in a magazine like *Rolling Stone* would be great for his headspace. He never asked for or craved attention or flattery, but I thought he'd enjoy it.

I called Wenner right back. "Okay, Jann, he'll give Anthony an hour. And tell him when I say an hour, I mean an hour, because if you let Curtis go, he'll talk for forever, and he doesn't need to expend the energy."

"Got it."

"And have Anthony send me his questions, so Curtis will be prepared."

"No problem."

"And Jann, no pictures. None whatsoever."

He paused. "What about a headshot?" he asked.

"No. Pictures. Period." Curtis didn't look deathly ill, but he didn't look well, and I was certain he wouldn't want his fans to see him in that state. "Use something from the archives."

"Okay, okay, fine, fine." It was obvious from his petulant tone that he wasn't happy, but he didn't fight me on it, because the article was too important.

"And Jann, don't fuck this up. I can't be there to watch over your guy. I'm trusting you."

"You have my word we'll do right by him."

The day before the interview, I called Curtis's wife, Althea, with Anthony's list of questions, then asked her to call me the second Anthony took off. Althea rang back the following afternoon: "Well, they just left."

"*They?*" I said. "What do you mean *they?*"

"The writer and the photographer."

"Wait a second. There was a *photographer?!*" I hadn't mentioned anything to Curtis or Althea about my discussion with Jann regarding photographs, figuring that when Wenner gave me his word, it meant something. "What did this photographer do?" I asked, trying to maintain my composure.

"Well, he stood up on a chair and took a couple of shots of Curtis lying in bed. I'm pretty sure Curtis's colostomy bag was in the frame."

"What did Curtis say about this?"

"Oh, you know Curtis. He never says no to anybody."

I got off the phone, counted to ten, then, once my blood stopped boiling, I called Jann. "Look, man," I said, "this is not a joke. When I said no pictures, I meant no pictures."

"Ronnie, I haven't even seen any of the shots. . . ."

I said, "Don't even bother looking at them. None of those pictures are going into your magazine."

Guess what: One of those pictures went into his magazine. A picture of Curtis in bed, colostomy bag in full view. The day the issue hit the stands, I received over twenty phone calls from the folks at Curtis's label, Warner Brothers, including three each from their president, Mo Ostin, and Rick Shoemaker, the head of Curtis's publisher, Warner/Chappell. The general sentiment was, "How the fuck could you let this happen, Weisner?" I didn't want to get into specifics, because I knew no one wanted to hear it, so I just told everyone, "I didn't authorize it. Curtis never says no. Wenner's an asshole. Period." There wasn't anything more to say, really.

This time, I didn't count to ten before I called Wenner. "Let me tell you something, you motherfucking prick. I will never do anything for you or with you ever again. And if I can get in the way of you doing something with anybody I deal with, I will go do it. I'm going to go out of my way to make your life miserable, you little cocksucker." And then I slammed down the phone. He never called me back.

The following year, I ran into Wenner at some industry schmooze-a-thon. Before he could escape, I grabbed him by the elbow and said, "Was that picture of Curtis necessary? Why would you do that to the guy? Why would you demean a great man like that?" Before he could answer, I gave him a shove and stomped off. I haven't seen nor spoken with Jann Wenner since.*

That whole situation left such a horrible taste in my mouth for years, so I wanted to do something to honor Curtis, both as a person and a musician. (Frankly, he needed it, because come 1994, he was seriously down; he'd never tell you he was down, but I could tell.) It dawned on me that there were probably dozens of artists who would cite him as a major influence and would be thrilled to pay him a musical tribute. I thought, *What about a tribute album? What if I round up the greatest of the great and have them cover Curtis's greatest songs?*

But before I could do anything, I had to get Curtis's okay, so I flew down to Roswell, because something like this required more than a phone call. After I explained my idea, I said, "If you don't want to, you don't have to do anything. I'd love to figure out a way for you to do a song, but there's absolutely no pressure." Curtis could still sing, but the only way he could get enough wind to do so was to lie flat on his back, and I knew he wasn't comfortable with that.

....

* Unsurprisingly, Curtis took the high road about the whole thing: "Maybe I shouldn't have let them take the picture," he told me, "but I didn't want to upset anybody."

He didn't say anything.

I continued. "I have some specific people in mind. Bruce Springsteen. Phil Collins. Whitney Houston. Lenny Kravitz. Gladys Knight. Steve Winwood."

Still nothing.

"It's a cross section of genres," I said. "I want to show how important you were to R&B *and* rock *and* pop *and* soul."

Finally, with a serious look on his face, he said, "Ron, why would these people do this for me? I don't deserve this. Who am I?"

Astounding. "Curtis, they'll want to do this because you mean something to them."

"I don't know. . . ."

Choking up, I said, "Curtis, let me ask you something. Do you trust me? Would I do anything to hurt you?"

"Of course I trust you. Of course you'd never hurt me."

"Then keep trusting me on this one. And think about if there's something you want to contribute, and if you do, we'll figure out a way to make it happen."

He sighed, then said, "Let me think about it tonight."

"No," I said, "you're going to tell me now. Because I know what's going to happen. You're going to come up with a hundred reasons why we shouldn't do it, and you're gonna sweet-talk me into agreeing with you. Tell me now, because I want this to happen for you. It's important for me personally that we do this. So let's do it."

After what seemed like forever, he said, "I trust you. Let's do it."

The next morning, I worked the phones, calling the acts directly, because in some cases managers just get in the way. Every single person I asked said yes, without a second thought. I wasn't surprised that they all agreed, but I was amazed how quickly they did so. Usually when you ask something of a Clapton or an Aretha, they'll say, "Hmmm, that's a great idea, and it sounds like a lot of fun, but I have a lot of stuff going on, so let me think about it for a couple of days and I'll get back to you," and maybe they'd get back to you, and maybe they wouldn't. But not this time. For Curtis, they were all willing to move mountains. (The only issue was the tune "Gypsy Woman," which Lenny, Phil, and Bruce all wanted to do. But Springsteen won that battle, because when he growled, *I have to do it*," well, I couldn't say no.)

Highlights included Rod Stewart's string-filled version of "People Get Ready," the Isley Brothers' super-slow rendition of "I'm So Proud," and B.B. King's shuffle take of "Woman's Got Soul." As for Curtis, well, in typical Curtis fashion, he wanted to please me, so he did a verse on a cover of "Let's Do It Again" from a group called the Repercussions, and damned if he didn't sound like his old self.

Later that year, the Grammy brain trust saw fit to give Curtis the Legend Award, and everyone who knew him desperately wanted him to be at the show. The problem was moving Curtis from Georgia to Los Angeles would be an expensive endeavor and a logistical quagmire, requiring doctors, nurses, and a medevac airplane. But Warner Brothers stepped up. Mo Ostin told Curtis, "We're going to do what we have to do to get you out there." True to his word, they paid for everything without a single complaint.

A couple weeks before he hit LA for the show, I told him, "Curtis, I want you to come to my house for dinner when you're out here. My kids would love to see you."

Without a moment's hesitation, Curtis said, "I'd be honored."

A few days before the Grammys, I was chatting with some of the musicians and industry types in town for the show, among them Philip Bailey and Maurice White from Earth, Wind & Fire, and my old friend Don Cornelius. Philip asked when Curtis was coming to town, and I told him, "A few days before the show. He'll need to rest up so he'll have enough energy to do his thing." And then, quite proudly, I said, "He's coming to my house the night before the show."

"I'd love to see him," Maurice said. Everyone agreed.

I thought, *What the hell,* then said, "Why don't you all come over for dinner? I'll ask a few other folks, and we'll make a night of it."

I invited eighteen people; sixty-five showed. And it was almost all musicians: Sting, Stevie Wonder, Whitney Houston, the list goes on. They just wanted to be close to him, to tell him what he meant to them, to be in his presence. During one of the brief moments he wasn't surrounded by well-wishers, he motioned me over and said, "I thought we were just gonna be having dinner with your family."

"Yeah, me too. But these cats followed you here. I couldn't stop them."

Curtis passed away at the end of 1999. On February 21, 2000, two days before that year's Grammy Awards ceremony, I hosted a memorial service for Curtis at the First African Methodist Episcopal Church. The band that performed at the service was mind-blowing: Stevie Wonder, Eric Clapton, Bill Withers, The Impressions, Gladys Knight. Yes, they were all in town for the Grammys, but I'm 100

Mrs. Curtis Mayfield and the Mayfield family cordially
invite you to a celebration of the life of Curtis Mayfield

Tuesday, February 22, 2000
12 noon
First African Methodist Episcopal Church of Los Angeles
2270 S. Harvard Blvd. Los Angeles, California 90018

Kindly RSVP by February 16, 2000 to Warner Bros.
818-953-2480 as seating is limited

Private invitation to the Curtis Mayfield memorial service

After Grammy party, lifetime achievement award for Curtis Mayfield. Gladys Knight, The Impressions, Narda Michael Walden, Marv Heiman, Lenny Warnoker, Mo Ostin, Frances Preston, Russ Teitleman, Charlie Feldman, Curtis Mayfield, Bonnie Raitt, Ron Weisner, and Steve Winwood.

percent certain that they'd have flown in from all over the world to pay homage to Curtis. For that matter, Stevie and Eric cancelled their Grammy performances, because they chose to play at the service rather than go to the Grammy rehearsal. Curtis was that beloved.

As I listened to these greats cover Curtis's best songs— as I listened to some of the best modern R&B I'd ever heard live and in person—I thought, "I'd give anything— *anything*—not to have had to do this." Because 99 percent of the time I was around Curtis Mayfield, everything was uplifting and good, and the other 1 percent was a learning experience. He was one of my favorite people in or out of the music industry, and I'm proud that I could call him my friend.

CHAPTER FIVE

Withers

For the last few decades, everyone and their mother has tried to get Bill Withers back in the studio, myself included, to no avail. But that won't stop me from trying again, and again, and again....

Clarence Avant was the man in charge of Sussex Records. He was based in Los Angeles, but he liked what he'd heard about our machinations in New York and Chicago, so he asked if we could help nurture his label. Who were we to say no?

After the hands were shaken and the papers were drawn up, he pulled a cassette tape from his pocket and said, "Mind if I stick this in? This is a guy I'm thinking about signing."

He popped and hit play. And then we heard The Voice.

There are some singing voices that can be relatively easily described—Janis Joplin is gravelly, Luther Vandross is honey-soaked, Billie Holiday is heart-wrenching—but others, words do not do justice. If you say the singer's name, that's enough.

This singer's name was Bill Withers.

Four bars into the first track, Neil said, "Clarence, if you don't sign this guy, you're a fucking idiot."

Clarence was anything but a fucking idiot, so the contracts were drawn up and inked. Between 1971 and 1974, Bill recorded three albums for Sussex, the first one of which featured "Ain't No Sunshine" and the second, "Lean On Me." Those two songs comprise six of the most enduring minutes in the history of modern popular music, songs that transcend age, race, or style. The fact that I was even peripherally involved with them will always be a point of pride.

Some artists are absolutely unlike their music; for example, Miles Davis. If you listen to Miles's classic live recording of "My Funny Valentine," and you hear the way he caresses the notes out of his trumpet, you'd probably think, "That is one beautiful soul." But the reality was that Miles was a cantankerous, unpredictable, sometimes violent man. Bill Withers, however, was just like his songs: understated, thoughtful, spiritual, laid-back, and classy.

Bill was also quite shy. He grew up in the tiny town of Slab Fork, West Virginia, a coal miner's town. When Clarence discovered him, he was living in Los Angeles, working for a place called Weber Aircraft in Burbank; after he went from being Bill Withers to BILL WITHERS, we often laughed about the fact that not more than a year before, he was making toilets for airplanes.

After his first album was in the can, Bill put together a band—which may not seem like a big deal, but if you've never done it before, well, it's not as simple as it sounds—and made himself available to do any and all promotional activities we needed. He performed a few shows at The Bitter End in New York (and that's a tiny club; can you imagine seeing Bill Withers at a place the size of a high school classroom?), went on a few television shows (Dick Cavett, in particular, loved him), and conducted several select magazine interviews with writers who were able to discuss the nuts and bolts of music (Bill wasn't the kind of person who wanted to talk about his favorite color or how much he enjoys walking on the beach).

Even though he was shy, Bill was so kind that if a stranger asked him about one of his songs, he'd offer a twenty-minute answer, because his desire to tell a story trumped his bashfulness. While he enjoyed performing, he intensely disliked touring. Even when he was winning Grammys and topping the charts, I used to think if he had his druthers, he'd be happy staying in LA, playing a show once every two months, and that's that. But he was so agreeable that he did what we needed him to do with little complaint . . . most of the time.

"Ain't No Sunshine" was nominated for a Grammy Award in 1972, and that year's ceremony was to be held in New York. I called him up in LA and said, "Bill, the Grammys are next week. You should probably go."

"Do I have to?"

"You're nominated for three awards. It would be a good idea if you were there."

"Fine. I'll fly in the day of the show."

"Great," I said. "We'll have a car get you at the airport and take you to the office, then we'll go to the show together." He arrived at our place empty-handed: no suitcase, no suit bag,

Cecil Holmes, Clarence Avant, Bill Withers, and Ronnie Mosley

no nothing, just the clothes on his back. "Bill," I asked, "did you bring a tux or anything?"

He just shrugged. So I dropped everything I was doing, and we hopped a cab to Barney's Boys Town (eventually they shortened the name of the store to Barney's, which was probably a good idea) and got him a nice suit, in which he seemed completely uncomfortable. The two of us arrived at the Felt Forum—I was his date—and headed for our seats; the second we sat down, he said, "How long do we have to stay?"

"Um, well, you're up for three awards. We should probably find out whether you won any of them."

Bill sighed. "Fine." Five minutes later: "How long do you think it'll be until my categories are announced?"

He'd been nominated for Best New Artist, Best Pop Male Vocalist, and Best Rhythm & Blues Song. "You're up for some pretty big awards, Bill. Probably not until near the end. I think we're here for the night, my friend."

He sighed again. Winning the Best R&B Song award probably made the evening a little more tolerable for him. But that was Bill. He didn't—and probably still doesn't—like it when people make a big to-do about him.

Bill never had a manager because he didn't like to be involved in anything that needed managing. Clarence gave him some advice along the way, and I took care of as many of his logistics as I could, but soon after I moved out to Los Angeles, he agreed that he needed some help, so in 1981 we formalized our relationship. Almost immediately after that, he made one of his *very* rare trips into the studio, joining saxophonist Grover Washington Jr. on "Just the Two of Us." The song was a massive success and put him back on the map—not that he was ever off the map, really—and it drove me nuts that he refused to make a new album.

"Just do a goddamn record," I told him at least twice a month. "You don't even have to tour. Your music is timeless, and everybody loves you, and you need to give your fans some new stuff. I can set it up with one phone call."

Time and again, he refused. Bill was perfectly content with his life and didn't need to make music. He was married to a lovely woman, with whom he had two grown children; his only work was buying, rehabbing, then reselling old homes. But I was persistent; at least twice a month, he told me thanks, but no thanks. I was never surprised, and I was never upset. That was just Bill being Bill, a good man who liked to keep to himself.

Bill Withers

In 2010, I was producing some shows for India.Arie. We fell into a conversation about music, and she said, "My hero is Bill Withers."

"I know Bill," I said, then gave her the thumbnail sketch of our history.

India hung on every word, then asked, "Do you think you could get him to come to one of my gigs?" She was doing a week at the House of Blues in Los Angeles.

Playing the big shot, I said, "I'll see what I can do," not knowing if I'd actually be able to convince Bill to leave the house. But I must've said something right to him, because the following evening, Bill and his wife, Marcia, came out to the show.

The View from Bill Withers

People who run their own businesses have a certain kind of energy, because they have to. They're self-starters and they have plenty of initiative, but sometimes they start pushing you in the back, and it can get annoying. Ron Weisner did it right.

I could tell from the get-go that Ron was a get-it-done kind of guy, both interesting and interested. He even took care of the nuts-and-bolts stuff that nobody else wanted to do. You never had to go looking for him; if he sensed you needed something, he'd just show up. He was the go-to guy, and nothing was beneath him.

In 1973 we were getting ready to record a live album at Carnegie Hall, and our guitar player's amplifier was making more noise than your mother-in-law after three glasses of wine. So Ronnie took it upon himself to run around Manhattan and make sure we had a new amp. See, he's a problem solver, and there aren't enough of those in the world.

He was always so kind to Curtis Mayfield, and that always touched me. After Curtis's accident, Ronnie got in touch with everybody he thought Curtis would like to speak with and let them know how to find Curtis.

My favorite Ronnie Weisner visual: His first grandchild had just been born, and he'd gone out and bought some baby shoes. As he sat at his desk trying to wrap the gift, I thought, *That's Ronnie. He's got all this stuff going on here at the office, and the most important thing to him are these baby shoes.* That's the Ronnie that I like. That's the Ronnie I'll remember.

As Bill chatted with India—who was beside herself with excitement—Marcia pulled me aside and said, "Ron, I want to thank you."

"Thank India," I said. "It was her idea."

"No, I'm thanking you, because this is the first time he's taken me on a date in two years."

Even though Bill isn't part of the music world, to me, he'll always be part of the music world. And certainly a part of *my* music world.

CHAPTER SIX

Sha Na Na

There were twelve of them, and they couldn't agree on what time it was, let alone on why their salary should be split equally.

At Buddah, we had little shame. If Neil, Cecil, or I found an act we thought could help build our company, we'd give them a shot, no matter what the other two thought, and no matter how simple (Kasenetz and Katz), obscure (Lord Burgess and His Sun Islanders), or god-awful (Elephant's Memory) they might have been. For better or worse, that became part of our reputation. People in the industry knew that we'd listen to any tape, or go see any show . . . especially if the guy who invited us was buying the drinks. That's why in 1968, when someone whose name is lost in the sands of time invited us to Max's Kansas City to check out a group of students from Columbia University called Sha Na Na, who liked to dress up in 1950s-type clothes and sing doo-wop, we went.

It sounded like a ridiculous concept—a tribute to a bygone era that was barely gone?—but the group had generated a lot of buzz, and if something was buzzing, Buddah would, at the very least, want to take a look. We went in skeptically, and we left blown away. It was unequivocally a great show—clever, heartfelt, and smart, something that could be enjoyed by kids, grown-ups, and senior citizens. Their 1950s-era harmonies were authentic, as was their choreography, clothing, and style. (The gold lamé suits were especially memorable.) They all made up names for themselves, like Jocko, Bowser, and Dirty Dan, which was at once silly and charming. Musically speaking, they were clearly influenced by Elvis, as well as groups like the Spaniels, the Danleers, and the El Dorados. They weren't copying or parodying the era; they were paying homage with sincerity, and that sense of sincerity ruled the day.

And the hipsters at Max's ate it up.

We went back to see them the next week, then the next week, then the next, and it soon became evident that we weren't the only label sniffing around. But we could tell that none of the other labels had an idea what to do with them. Their songs were terrific, but would a record buyer or a radio listener be able to differentiate them from any other 1950s doo-wop group? Probably not. Their stage show defined them, but this was well before there were any television shows that would give them the kind of exposure that would translate into record sales. And as there were twelve members in the group, putting them on the road would've been an expensive proposition.

None of that fazed us. We pursued them, and while we didn't outbid their other suitors, we outhustled them. There was nothing else like Sha Na Na out there, and there was nothing else like Buddah out there; it seemed like a good match. Once the ink on the contract was dry, we sat down with the band and their manager, Ed Goodgold, a bright, witty twenty-five-year-old who could've passed for fifty. All of us agreed that we shouldn't try to turn them into something they weren't, so we had them cut a live album on their home turf of Columbia.

The record was a solid piece of material, but the music didn't work as well without the moves and the clothes. We knew we had to get them on the road, or they'd be dismissed as a novelty act, plus their show was a blast. If you didn't have a good time at a Sha Na Na concert, you needed to get your fun gene checked out. I was the Buddah point person for Sha Na Na—actually, I was the Buddah point person for most of our acts—and dealt with them on a daily basis, and between all of us, we managed to turn a quirky little niche group into a viable show business entity.

Credit where credit is due, those guys worked hard, to the tune of 250 shows a year. They played every damn college up and down the East Coast, they landed spots on television, and they hustled. Considering how badly they got along, we were always surprised that we didn't get a phone call from, say, a representative of the Cherry Hill, Delaware, sheriff's department asking us if we knew anything about the dead guy in the river with the greasy hair and the gold lamé jacket lodged up his ass.

On more than one instance, they duked it out before they took the stage. (On the plus side, watching a bunch of pretentious Columbia kids dressed like minor league James Deans awkwardly punching each other was amusing as

Sha Na Na and the Palace Guard in London, England

hell.) I often had to break it up; what usually put the kibosh on the scuffle was me telling them, "If you guys don't get your shit together, they'll cancel the show, and if they cancel the show, you won't get paid." That almost always ended the fight . . . for the time being. Sometimes they waited until after the show to beat the shit out of each other.

What set them off more than anything—even more than their natural dislike of one another—were discussions about repertoire. When they needed to add a song to the show, it inevitably devolved into World War III. This one thought he should sing lead, and the other one thought he should sing lead, and yet another one thought *he* should sing lead, and next thing you know, fisticuffs ensued. I never wanted to get involved in that shit, but sometimes I'd get pulled in. One of them would ask me, "What do you think?" and I'd say, "I think I'm leaving," then look for the closest exit.

One day soon after we signed Sha Na Na, and soon before their record was released, Neil called me into his office and said, "I have a family thing this weekend, so I need you to go upstate and cover this festival thing for me. Melanie and Sha Na Na are playing, and we need a presence. The thing starts on Friday, so rent a car on Thursday, drive up there in the morning, and take care of them."

"What show?"

He handed me a piece of paper. "Here's all the information. I'm sure it won't be a big deal."

I looked at the paper, then asked, "Where the fuck is Woodstock?"

Neil shrugged. "Fuck if I know. Upstate, I guess."

Thursday morning, I rented a car, tracked down a map, and hit the road. The closer I got to Woodstock, the thicker the traffic became. I thought, *Man, if it's this nuts the day before the thing starts, what's it gonna be like tomorrow?* Eventually, after winding my way through the clogged single-lane country roads, I parked in the far end of the area that had been designated as the parking lot, right by an area that I designated as a forest. I made the long walk from my car to the festival's stage area; as I looked back to where I'd just come from, all I could see was the masses streaming toward us and a picket fence surrounding the field that I suspected wouldn't last much longer.

Even though it was getting late, things were hopping in the behind-the-stage area, what with the musicians, their managers, the record label types, the production people, and the hangers-on all milling about, trying to lock down their credentials or score some drugs. While trying to get my bearings, I ran into one of our neighbors from 1650 Broadway, an energetic young man named Michael Lang.

I didn't know Michael well, just enough to say, "Hey howya doin'" in the hallway, but I gave him a big hello, because it was nice to see a friendly face in this sea of strangers. I asked him, "What're you doing here?"

Michael looked taken aback. "This is my thing. I'm producing this."

"No shit," I said.

"No shit."

"Congratulations. Any idea if I'll be able to get back to town and get to my hotel?"

He chuckled, said, "Good luck," and walked away.

With no way to get to a bed, I crashed in one of the big production trailers, alongside dozens of other exhausted, travel-weary industry types who'd also had no idea what they were getting into. A couple hours later, the skies opened, and we were treated to a torrential downpour that lasted for hours. Eventually the rain let up and the sun came out. At dawn, I tiptoed out of the trailer so as not to wake up anyone and stepped outside. In the brightness, I squinted like Mr. Magoo until my eyes adjusted to the light and took in the scene: people as far as the eye could see, all completely covered with mud. There were dozens of production people out in the field, laying down stacks of grass in order to keep the mud at bay. Others were skittering around the stage, attempting to plug the leaks and fix the equipment that had been damaged by the wind. I looked back out toward the growing audience, and, sure enough, there went the picket fence. It was like the dam broke. Thousands upon thousands spilled onto the field, immediately destroying the newly laid grass. *Man*, I thought, *I'm sure as hell glad to be on this side.**

Melanie was one of the last acts on the opening night, and Sha Na Na was the second to last performance of the festival, but I was there the whole time, because there was no way I was getting off the grounds. Hell, my chances of getting back to my car were pretty slim.

It was so impossible to get out of there that on Monday morning Lang's people arranged for helicopters to airlift the VIPs (and the less-than-VIPs like me) to a town far enough away where we could circumvent the crowd, rent a car, and get back to New York City. So I said a distant goodbye to my rental car, hopped the first copter, and made my way back home.

The next morning, Neil's assistant asked me, "Ron, did you return the rental car?"

I said, "Are you kidding? I haven't seen it since last Thursday. That thing is probably buried in a pile of mud by the woods."

"How are we gonna get it back?" she asked.

"Not my problem," I said, then went back to work.

....

* That is, until I saw all the topless girls. Then I wouldn't have minded being on the other side.

Over the next few years, Sha Na Na toured incessantly, periodically appeared on television, and constantly fought. When you have a dozen creative guys with a dozen visions of how their band should be presented, and a dozen opinions on who's the star of the show, there are going to be arguments. (You know how much Noel and Liam Gallagher argued? Well, multiply that by six, and you have a night on the road with Sha Na Na.) But they managed to pull it together onstage, and they were hard workers who brought in a nice chunk of change. I legitimately enjoyed watching their shows, so when I left Buddah and relocated to California, I became their manager.

Soon after, I landed them parts in the movie *Grease*, both on screen and on the soundtrack, and that catapulted them to another level entirely. So the wheels started turning, and I made a call to Pierre Cossette.

Pierre was a burly French-Canadian who was the go-to producer for the Grammy Awards. I liked the guy, he had a production company, and he was a music nut, so I pitched him an idea: a weekly variety show starring Sha Na Na.

He was skeptical. "How about we do a one-hour special?"

"This isn't a one-off," I said. "These guys are cartoon characters. It could be *Saturday Night Live* meets *Sesame Street*, and something like that won't be nearly as impactful if it's on once. It's a character-driven show with great music. It needs time to develop. We get some quirky guest stars, we get some good writers, and *boom*, we'll have a hit. Just come watch a concert, and we'll talk." I don't know if it was because the band's performance blew him away, or if I simply wore him down, but he got on board.

Things moved quickly. We landed a deal with a syndication company called Lexington Broadcast Services Company, but we still needed a sponsor. Pierre had a relationship with Procter & Gamble, who, at that point, was spending most of its ad bucks on laundry-oriented products. His team tried to sell P&G's people on Sha Na Na, but the P&G team didn't understand what the band or the show was about, so he insisted they come to a gig, because after they saw a performance, it would all make sense.

After that meeting, Pierre called me and asked whether we had any dates lined up anywhere near P&G's main offices in Cincinnati.

"Nope," I said, "just the usual college stuff."

"There's nothing special on the schedule?"

"Well, they're playing at Madison Square Garden. . . "

"Perfect!"

". . . as part of a 1950s revival show. It's a bunch of actual groups from the '50s."

"Oh."

I pointed out, "But they're closing the show, so it's kind of like they're the headliner."

"Okay, great," Pierre said, then called and invited the P&G decision makers to New York for the show. A couple days later, he called to tell me it was a go. "Now all you have to do is figure out a way to convince P&G that the band owns New York."

I thought about it for a second, then said, "Piece of cake. When're they getting into town?"

"The day before the show."

"What time?"

"Noon-ish."

"What airport?"

"Kennedy."

"Great. Call you back in a bit." I hung up, then rang up a billboard company, a few Teamsters, and a former NYPD detective, after which I called Pierre back. "Here's the deal," I said. "Have your people pick them up at the airport in a limo, then drive into Manhattan, and have the driver head north down Sixth beginning at 30th Street at exactly 2:45. Then tell him to drive uptown five blocks *very* slowly."

"Why?"

"I set it up so every billboard they see during that five-block ride will have a huge picture of Sha Na Na." Suddenly, we had a sponsor. Best $1,300 I ever spent.*

Next thing we know, we were on the air, with a street set that looked like it was pulled from an early greaser film, welcoming guest stars like Bernadette Peters, Little Richard, Rita Moreno, and Edgar Bergen and Charlie McCarthy, all of whom were "driven" onto the show by comedian Avery Schreiber in his fake taxi cab.

Over the show's four seasons on air, the band continued to work, and between the TV appearances and *Grease,* the shows were bigger, better, and stronger, both in and out of the United States. One week they'd be in Las Vegas, opening for Bill Cosby, and the next, they'd be at a festival in England or a small club in Japan. In the midst of all this activity, two of the guys left, and the remaining ten voted

----

* Two weeks later, I received an enormous box from P&G, filled with five hundred sample-size bottles of Scope mouthwash and one thousand sample packets of Bounce.

Sha Na Na on television show set

not to replace them, because twelve pieces of a single pie are smaller than ten. And Sha Na Na liked their pie.

By the time the TV show was cancelled in 1981, I'd moved on, in part because it was time, and in part because Michael happened.

CHAPTER SEVEN

The Jacksons

The Jackson Five were cute kids. When they grew up, well . . .

It seemed like I'd known Freddy DeMann forever. During my Buddah years, he lived in New York and was a promotion guy at various labels, most notably Elektra Records. We'd run into each other here and there, because most everyone who worked in the industry seemed to run into each other here and there. I wouldn't classify us as friends, but we were friendly enough that he confided in me his concern that Elektra was going to restructure, and he was going to lose his job, and he didn't know what he'd do next. I wasn't surprised Elektra was considering letting him go. While quite good at his job and a good guy, he was an opinionated guy, and I was certain he'd ruffled a few feathers during his tenure.

Sure enough, soon after I moved to California, his tenure at Elektra came to an end—I don't know if he was fired, or if he quit, or if it was a mutual decision—and he migrated west. As was the case in New York, our paths crossed every so often, and when they did, we had the kind of pleasant, insubstantial conversations you'd have with a casual acquaintance in your industry. Eventually, he started calling me on a regular basis, asking if I'd be interested in bringing him into my management company.

Initially, I was resistant to work with anyone at all. I was doing well with Curtis Mayfield, Gladys Knight, and Sha Na Na, among others. Everyone on my roster was regularly and successfully touring and recording, the business was smooth, and I was a happy guy, proud of the choices I'd made and optimistic about the future. Sure, in the back of my mind, I imagined that I'd someday have a bigger roster filled with creative, eager artists who had the potential and the desire to change the musical world, or at least have a long, fruitful career.

But Freddy was a great promotion guy, experienced, energetic, and aggressive. Plus I knew him, so I said what the hell, and Ron Weisner Entertainment became Weisner/DeMann Entertainment.

Before we made it official, I explained to him that my artists were my artists. "Gladys and those crazy Sha Na Na guys aren't part of the pot. The acts we sign together are ours, and we split those down the middle." He agreed, and off we went.

One of the first acts we signed together was Tavares, a good-natured family R&B band from Boston who had a couple hits with "Heaven Must Be Missing an Angel" and "It Only Takes a Minute." But they didn't go to the next level because that wasn't their priority. They all had families and weren't willing to spend every waking hour touring and promoting. And I respected that. If your heart isn't into it 100 percent, you're not going to be happy, and if you're not happy, your music and concerts will reflect that, and you'll eventually go into the crapper. Tavares chose their fate, and for that, they get points.

From our perspective, that was problematic, as they didn't make us any money, and I knew that Gladys and Sha Na Na couldn't sustain us forever. So that's why in the middle of 1977, when my friend Kate called me up and said, "I have some folks I'd like to introduce you to. It's a singing group. They're having problems. I think you can help," I immediately asked, "What kind of help?"

"*Your* kind of help."

That told me one thing: Their sales were in the shitter, and they needed someone to turn it around. I could do that. "What singing group?" I asked.

She paused. "I don't know how you're going to feel about it. They're tough."

Intrigued, I asked, "How tough?"

"*Real* tough. There are, shall we say, personalities involved. And career-wise, things are not going well for them."

I knew it. "Define 'not going well.'"

"Their sales are in the shitter."

Right again. "Okay. Define 'personalities.'"

Another pause. "For the most part, the boys in the group are okay. The guy in charge is. . . ." And then she drifted off.

"The guy in charge is what?" I asked.

"He's difficult."

"How difficult?"

Yet another pause. "The word *nightmare* has been tossed around."

"By who?"

"Let's see, the label, promoters, managers, family, friends, and, um, me. But you get along with everybody. Like I said, I think you can help."

And that was my introduction to Joe Jackson and his sons Randy, Marlon, Jackie, Tito, and Michael.

The Jackson Five were the original boy band, but unlike, say, One Direction, who was created by producer Simon Cowell, or the Backstreet Boys, who were created by entrepreneur Lou Pearlman, the Jacksons were created by a relative, the aforementioned nightmare, their father, Joe. For all his faults—and there are lots and lots of faults—Joe knew how to get his sons to make some great music, so in 1968, after four years of playing state fairs around their native Indiana, they signed with Motown Records, for whom they recorded twelve albums, which spawned countless hit singles. While all five of the brothers were uniquely talented, it was obvious to even the casual listener that the star was the youngest, Michael. Had Michael not become a teenage heartthrob, it's questionable as to whether the group would have survived after they left Motown. But come 1976, when they moved over to Epic Records, they were still a viable entity . . . just not as viable as they used to be, which is something that few cared to admit. (Post-Motown, they were called the Jacksons rather than the Jackson Five, because Motown owned their original name.)

The View from Gladys Knight

Everybody thinks Diana Ross discovered the Jackson Five, but—and this is nothing against her—Diana wasn't the kind of girl who'd go to a club and check out other artists. Diana was about Diana. She wasn't out there looking for talent.

I was in my dressing room at the Regal Theater in Chicago, and the Pips and I were getting ready to do our show as part of a Motown review. Like the Apollo Theater, the Regal had an amateur show, and there was a rehearsal onstage for the next night's amateur hour. And then I heard this voice.

I stopped what I was doing, got out of my chair, and said aloud, "Who is that? Who is that?!" I went upstairs and peeked over the banister. The group was way downstage, so I couldn't really see them. But I heard them and said, "Oh my goodness," then went back to the dressing room. The Pips knew everybody, so I said, "Who were those boys up there on the stage? Those kids were amazing."

My brother Bubba said, "Those're Joe's boys. Joe Jackson. He's always talking about his boys, always trying to make it happen."

I said, "I want to meet them."

Bubba said, "I'll tell Joe."

After their rehearsal, they came up to the dressing room, and they were soooo cute. Michael was so little that when he sat on the sofa, his feet didn't even touch the floor. And you know what I loved most about them? They were so vulnerable and respectful, and they had this wonderful energy about them. We talked for a while, and they all left . . . except for Michael. He was full of questions: "How do you feel about being in the business? When you sing for a big crowd, what do you feel? How do you keep your voice healthy?" Even at that young age, Michael was an inquisitive prodigy.

If you weren't Diana, or Smokey, or sometimes the Temptations, you didn't have a lot of pull at Motown, so I had to ask our label manager, Mr. Cox, to get me in touch with Berry Gordy. When he asked why, I told him that I had a group for them to sign, and they needed to do it yesterday. When he said, "Okay, okay, we'll get back to you," I told him, "You REALLY have to get back to me! Don't push me off. You're our manager, and you're supposed to get things done for us, and we don't ask you for much, so find Mr. Gordy and let him know that I need to talk with him!"

Mr. Gordy never called, so I called Mr. Cox again the next morning and said, "Look, you need to get Mr. Gordy to come and see this group. That's the only way I can get my point across. That's the only way he'll be able to tell how amazing they are. If he can't come, you come. We're in Chicago, and that's only a four-hour drive from Detroit, and forty-five minutes if you fly!"

He said, "Okay, okay, I'll get down there." He never came.

When I got back to Detroit, I tried to tell everybody about the Jacksons, and nobody would listen. Honestly, a lot of them were too wrapped up in themselves, so I couldn't get anybody to budge. It took a lot of phone calls and harassment on my part, but Mr. Gordy finally heard their tape, and the rest is history.

To be honest, hooking the Jacksons to Diana's star was the smartest thing that Motown could have done. At that time, the press liked drama, and I was a goody-two-shoes, so there wasn't anything dramatic about me.

Another thing I appreciated from Ron was that he kept me and Michael together. Michael only surrounded himself with people he was comfortable with, and he loved Ron Weisner. So when Michael and Ron were in whatever town I was in, Ron would call and say, "Michael's here," and I'd say, "I'll be right over." When I'd get there, the three of us would sit on the floor and talk for hours. And just like when he was a kid, Michael asked me crazy questions about life, and music, and the business, and family. Those were the kind of questions a young boy would ask, and I always thought of him as a young boy, even when he became a man.

It's that childlike quality that made his music so pure. Ron always told me, "Michael isn't like the rest of us," and he was exactly right.

The brothers' first two post-Motown albums, *The Jacksons* and *Goin' Places,* were solid records, but, relatively speaking, they stiffed. They did nothing. (*Nothing* may seem like an exaggeration, but compared to the numbers they were putting up at Motown, *nothing* is an apt adjective.) Their lack of transcendence was due in part to the fact that the Jacksons were making the awkward transition from cute little kids to young adults, and the music, for the most part, didn't reflect their maturity. They were viewed as the all-American family, but songs like "Living Together" from *The Jacksons* and "Man of War" from *Goin' Places* seemingly weren't appealing to listeners who grew up on the poppish, sanitized sounds of "ABC" and "Rockin' Robin." They had a flavor-of-the-month vibe, but their month spun out into years, and by the mid-1970s, those years were over.

Another cause for their career stagnation: Joe. Dad was steering the ship—and not steering it well. I did some research, and the word on the street was that he was a street guy, a hustler, not exactly personality-plus. He was their manager but didn't really manage them; he wasn't creative, he wasn't a businessperson, he was just their father, and he was there to make money. He pushed his sons to the limit in terms of rehearsing and performing, sucking every last drop of energy out of them in order to pad his pockets. Everyone I spoke to said he was difficult to deal with, that he ruled his family with an iron fist, that it was his way or no way. Across the board, those who had worked with him in the past had called him rude or arrogant and had little or no interest in working with him again. Suzanne DePasse, Berry Gordy's former assistant, told me that the kids were great to deal with, but Joe was a completely untrustworthy nightmare, and Bob Jones, the group's old PR person at Motown, gave me a few horror stories of his own. And Suzanne and Bob weren't the only ones with scary tales— there were ten others. When twelve people tell you the same thing, well, let's just say you don't need to go looking for number thirteen. So I knew I was walking into a minefield . . . but I walked anyhow.

The Jacksons' less-than-stellar sales led to less-than-stellar bookings, then the less-than-stellar bookings led to no bookings. Unless things turned around, and turned around quick, they were doomed to return to Indiana and work the state fair circuit, playing "I'll Be There" and "Rockin' Robin" for a bunch of people who were more interested in their cotton candy than music. It was clear to me that with a lot of work and a solid game plan, the Jackson brothers could be salvaged . . . that is, if they could overcome their greatest obstacle: their father.

Our first meeting was at my office and consisted of me, Joe, Freddy, and our mutual friend Kate. What with his big rings, his flashy chains, and his hat that was five sizes too small for his head, he *looked* like a hustler. He explained that he was searching for a co-manager for his boys, but only a *co*-manager, because he wanted to maintain as much control as possible. As he questioned me, I felt not like I was being interviewed, but rather auditioned, which was off-putting, because I knew that he knew and respected Gladys Knight, and I was certain that he grilled her about me, and I was doubly certain that she said nothing but nice things. You'd think that Gladys's endorsement would lead to a more genial, respectful attitude from him. But you'd think wrong.

When I broached the topic of money, he got cagey, refusing to divulge his own cut before magnanimously saying, "My boys are willing to pay you guys 15 percent." I thought, *Um, that's nice, Joe, because that's how much anyone pays any manager these days.*

As for Joe's demeanor, at first he was on his best behavior throughout, keeping his natural crankiness *mostly* under wraps, but as the afternoon rolled on, he became more and more contentious, saying, "I got these problems with the record company, and they ain't likin' me a whole lot, so I need *me* a white guy to deal with *their* white guys."

Freddy and I just looked at each other. I mean, what do you say?

As an uncomfortable silence stretched on, it dawned on me that he didn't need a white guy to talk to their white guys; he needed a nice, sane, respectable guy to talk to their white guys. CBS probably hated dealing with Joe, and Joe knew it.

Being that I'm a nice, sane, respectable guy, I didn't say, *Joe, how much does CBS hate you,* but rather I asked, "Joe, what do your kids want out of us?"

"Ask 'em yourself," he snapped. "We'll get together at the house." And that was the end of that meeting. Joe's antagonistic, surly attitude made me nervous . . . but not nervous enough that I didn't want to see how it all played out.

Even though the Jacksons had high visibility and an existing fan base, this was going to be one of the biggest challenges of my career, even more challenging than trying to keep the Sha Na Na guys from murdering each other. For some reason, it's always been more difficult to resurrect the career of a once-successful act that's bottomed out than it is to break a new one. It would require mending fences with label personnel and promoters and assembling just the right team of writers and producers. (I had some specific writers and producers in mind, but I didn't name names, because I was concerned that Joe would go behind my back and track them down himself.) It would require change and compromise, something that's always a touchy subject with a client—or, more saliently, a *prospective* client—because some creatives translate compromise as selling out. To me, compromise equals taking your existing puzzle pieces and combining them with new and different puzzle pieces that you might not have known even existed, then piecing them together into something that you can be proud of and the public will appreciate. Some balk at that, and I understand. Artists in any venue have a certain vision—if they didn't have vision, they wouldn't be interested in being an artist in the first place—and if their only goal is to realize that vision, more power to them . . . but that vision might not be commercially viable. I have nothing but respect for those who want to create their version of the perfect song, or the perfect book, or the perfect sculpture, with no regard for form, structure, or what has appealed to the masses in the past. But they have to understand and accept that a record label, or a publisher, or an art dealer probably won't agree with their view of perfect, so their work of art might never see the light of day beyond the artist's living room. However, if you tap into your natural talent, examine and absorb the business and aesthetic climate of the day, create from your heart, and play well with others, your chances of climbing the mountain are greatly improved.

The next week, I explained all of this to the boys, and they seemed energized, ready to make changes, ready to take this new journey wherever it might lead. They came across as hungry, especially Michael, whose craving for acceptance and adulation was palpable. He said, "Let's find songs. Let's find producers. Let's put together a hit record.

Let's go on the road." Joe then left the room, after which Michael leaned forward and said, "We don't want Joseph dealing with the record company." (For as long as I've known them, none of the Jacksons have ever referred to Joe as Dad, or Daddy, or "our father." It was always Joseph.) "Our records didn't sell enough, and nobody wants to deal with him."

"I'll do my best." I hoped I could keep Joe at bay and fix what had been broken; the brothers didn't deserve to have their careers destroyed by a clueless relative, because they were good kids and talented as hell. When they were into it, they were the best. Their steps, while not as meticulously choreographed as those you'll see from the dancers at, say, a Beyoncé concert, were charming in their looseness. And those Jacksons could flat-out sing. No backing tracks, just five guys harmonizing like they'd been doing it together for their entire lives . . . which they had. Their concerts as a whole flowed brilliantly—it merely wasn't one song, then the next, then the next, but rather an honest-to-goodness show that showed off both their collective skills and personae. There was no evident ego. They were a team whose sole goal was to give you a night to remember, a lesson they'd learned while part of the Motown Records stable. And Kate was right: They were good kids.

A quick digression: Motown had terrific choreographers and costume stylists on staff, so the label's stable of artists would always be in step and look good; when I managed Gladys Knight, we worked with a great, talented, old-school choreographer out of the Motown School named Cholly Atkins, and that man knew what he was doing. I regularly watched Cholly put Gladys and the Pips through their drills, and it's no wonder the Motown artists uniformly looked terrific onstage. He was a kindly taskmaster who'd clearly studied the great black dancers from the 1940s, like the Nicholas Brothers (masters of the Flying Splits, and if you haven't seen that particular move, put this book down and visit YouTube), John "Bubbles" Sublett, and Bill "Bojangles" Robinson, and preached moving, and timing, and energy. You knew that if the Jackson Five, or the Temptations, or the Four Tops were onstage or in front of the camera, you'd see a class performance.

Another quick digression: You also had the chitlin circuit, where, in terms of stage presentation, all bets were off. From the 1950s all the way up to the late 1970s, the majority of the hardcore R&B audience was situated in the South, so if a singer or group wanted to make money, they'd put together a club tour below the Mason-Dixon Line. The tours were quick and dirty—they'd go from one city to the next with very little rest, playing joints that, while homes to loyal audiences, weren't bright and shiny, but rather dingy and raucous. And the music and performances reflected the low-rent aspect of things. Down on the circuit, you wouldn't see much in the way of unison dance steps, or matching outfits, or polish. We're talking loose, boisterous, and fun. It was the perfect situation for an artist to hone his or her performing chops, because the audiences were predisposed to appreciate, rather than criticize.

In any event, thanks to Motown—and, of course, the brothers' natural talent—if you bought a ticket to a Jackson Five concert, you were guaranteed a night of sheer entertainment. On the way to the parking lot, the one thing you'd hear time and again was, "Wow, we had *fun* tonight. We had a great time."

Fortunately, in 1978, we were able to capture that sense of play on vinyl with *Destiny*. Our A&R guys on that album were Bobby Colomby and Paul Atkinson, and even though they were employees of Epic Records, they weren't Suits, and thus were people we could all respect. Aside from the fact that he was a musician himself—his highest-profile gig was as the drummer for Blood, Sweat & Tears—Bobby was enthusiastic, and positive, and he had great ears. And he knew the problems regarding the Jacksons' standing within the label all too well. "I like those kids," he told me right before we started recording *Destiny*, "but when Joe's around, they're different people. They're uncomfortable, they're nervous, they never speak up about anything. There're a lot of people up here who think they're more trouble than they're worth. This record needs to be big, or . . . " He didn't finish the thought, assuming correctly that I knew what "or" meant.

We all spent a lot of time and energy figuring out what musicians would best bring the music to life, eventually deciding that we shouldn't overthink things and just hire the best, because—and I've found this to be more true in the music world than anywhere else—you have to spend money to make money. The great Claire Fischer delivered some beautiful string arrangements, and the great Jerry Hey did the same for the horns. And our rhythm sections, featuring heavyweights like guitarist Michael Sembello, bassist Nathan Watts, and drummer Ricky Lawson, were uniformly rock solid.

The View from Bobby Colomby

The Jacksons didn't have any advocates at the label. Their two records hadn't done well, they were a Saturday morning cartoon show, and they weren't very highly thought of. I had a whole different perspective. I saw potential, so I put in the time and effort.

The band wanted to produce the record themselves, but they didn't really have the qualifications, but I wanted to find a way to get them as much credibility as possible. Joe Jackson told me that they wouldn't record any of their original compositions unless they owned the publishing rights in their entirety. I found that extremely offensive, in light of the fact that they were struggling so badly. But that was Joe.

In his nurturing way, Bobby leaned on the brothers to concoct some material that could be heard on the radio for months and heard on dance floors for years. Because the brothers were the same ages as their demographic, their creative input was invaluable, certainly more useful and welcome than when they were with Motown. (Actually, Stevie Wonder was pretty much the only Motown artist who had any kind of creative control.) This was a considerably different approach than they took with *The Jacksons* and *Goin' Places*; I felt that they didn't offer too many musical suggestions because (a) they thought they could get by on their name and history alone, and (b) nobody asked. Much to everyone's delight, Michael and Randy came up with

"Shake Your Body," which landed in the *Billboard* Top Ten, and Bobby brought in the other hit from the album, "Blame It on the Boogie," a tune cowritten by a couple of Englishmen with the last name of Jackson.

It should be noted that when the brothers were recording, Joe rarely visited the studio. Why? Because he didn't give a shit about the music. His only concern was that the album be completed so he could make his money. (It's ironic that Joe wasn't around, because the studio, Hollywood Sound, was in the sleaziest part of Hollywood—you couldn't walk outside without tripping on a hooker. You'd think a guy like Joe would be right at home in that sort of neighborhood.) His sole contributions to the album were periodic complaints that the sidemen were being overpaid. I, however, visited the studio on a regular basis, and it was clear that the brothers didn't want him around anyhow, proving Colomby was right: Without Joe, they were freer, more relaxed, and, most important, better performers. I think that's why they were always happy to see me and Freddy—we were a breath of fresh air. Plus we weren't Joe. (The CBS marketing and promotions people were just as happy. A promo person who shall remain nameless told me, "Finally, there's some sanity with this project. Finally, we have someone we can talk to.")

Joe was invisible at the studio, but he always wanted to be there for the business meetings, something I tried hard to discourage, because when he was around, no matter what topic was up for a discussion, he'd go off on an angry, hostile rant: "You white boys don't know shit! These're my goddamn kids! I make the decisions! Nothin's gonna happen without me!"

Despite Joe's unwitting efforts to sabotage his sons' career, *Destiny* was a smash. It went multiplatinum, and just like that, the Jacksons were back to life. Much of the industry, and a huge number of fans, had written them off as a kid group who lacked the skill set necessary to make quality grown-up music. Man, they were wrong. That album sounds great to this day. For that matter, unlike the vast majority of records released in 1978, it doesn't feel the least bit dated.

The two most important results of the record were (a) it put the Jacksons back in the public eye, and (b) it crossed over onto white radio. That being the case, the impending shows were make-or-break endeavors, thus they had to be brilliant. In terms of the size of the venues, we took a con-servative approach, forgoing 15,000-plus-seat arenas for 4,000-seat sheds. I wanted to build from the bottom, to cre-ate a buzz, and if people had trouble getting tickets, well, that sent a better message than barely filled arenas. Besides, if the show sold out, we could always add a date—which was exactly what happened on several instances during the tour—and that sends the best message of all. Joe naturally balked at this plan, because fewer seats meant less money for the band, and less money for the band meant less off-the-top money in his pocket. When he voiced his complaints with the boys, I told them, "We shouldn't bite off more than we can chew. You guys haven't had a hit record in years, so let's *build*. And let's keep everything under our control. Let's control our destiny." (They liked the part about destiny, especially Michael.) The brothers were convinced, so Joe had to go along with the plan, whether he wanted to or not.

If the gigs were both of high quality and sold out, we could carry that momentum into the next record, and the next, and the next. If the shows were lousy and the venues were half-filled, we'd be worse off than we were when we started, so when it came to prepping for the tour, I felt I needed to be hands-on. The label wasn't going to provide any help, and Joe—if he bothered to show up, which we all knew wasn't going to happen—would've screwed things up, so unless I wanted to leave them to their own devices, I had no choice. Fortunately, they liked having me around. They came to trust me and asked for my opinions on a regular basis. Sometimes they agreed with me, sometimes they disagreed, and sometimes there were heated discussions, but even in the midst of an argument, I could tell they liked having me around, because they knew I had their back.

They also liked that I was really, really good at keeping Joe away. Sure, he stopped by once in a while, but he didn't stay for long because the boys had stopped listening to his creative input, such as it was, so there was nothing for him to do. Sometimes he'd show up with some strangers in tow, and they inevitably sat there until one of the brothers— usually Michael—said, "Ron, could you clear the room? Except you. You can stay." (None of them had the balls to tell Joe that he should leave, choosing to go for that passive-aggressive shit.) I was happy to kick him out, because all he did was bring the brothers down and piss me off.

The brothers were so jazzed by the whole thing that they dived into rehearsals for the tour with a sense of passion that at once surprised and impressed me. None of them slacked for a second; they spent as much time as necessary to get everything just right, and they never settled for anything less. Michael was especially intense about achieving perfection. Despite the fact that he was the second youngest guy in the band—he used to be the youngest, but Randy replaced Jermaine because Jermaine married Berry Gordy's daughter, which created some drama that I chose to avoid—in his quiet way, he was the group's driving creative force.

But if you sat down and had a serious musical talk with Michael Jackson, you'd understand why he was so eager to deliver such fun shows and equally fun albums—because he studied not just singers but entertainers, and he studied hard. His four favorites: Fred Astaire, Charlie Chaplin, James Brown, and Jackie Wilson. Those people—a dancer who sang, an actor who danced and sang, a shouter who danced, and a singer who glided—were Michael's gods, and they were inside of him, on a certain level, at all times . . . and especially while the Jacksons were on this particular tour.

Michael, for a while, was petrified to fly, which meant that for our first two tours with the Jacksons, we rode a bus, and you haven't lived until you've done a bus tour in an old tour bus. Tour buses, circa 1980, weren't the high-end luxury European-style buses you see today, buses replete with soft bunks, cushy chairs, satellite televisions, video games, bathrooms, and microwave ovens. They were buses, period. You had some seats, you had a few bunks, you had a ten-inch black-and-white television, a cassette player, and, if you were lucky, a video player. On the tours in question, we had multiple buses; the brothers and I rode in Bus #1, while the sound and scenery crew were in Bus #2. We had a VHS, which Michael commandeered after shows, and he played homemade tapes featuring performances from Astaire, Chaplin, Brown, and Wilson. Michael stared at the tiny TV, enraptured by these entertainers, sometimes inspired to the point that he'd mimic their dance steps in the aisle of the bus.

After a couple hours of this, Randy, or Marlon, or whoever, would stomp down to the front of the bus and menacingly tell Michael, *"Enough!"*

Generally, Michael just giggled, which enraged his brothers, so whichever one happened to be the most pissed off on any particular night would remove the video from the player and threaten to break it. Michael then freaked out to the point of tears, so they could never bring themselves to destroy the tape. It should be noted that Michael's brothers weren't nearly as dedicated to their craft as he was. They'd show up to rehearsal on time, and they'd do what they had to do, but they weren't ones for any kind of extracurricular study. Conversely, Michael wouldn't stop studying, his thinking being that he needed all of this history in his blood so he could work his audiences into a frenzy. His energy level back then was off the charts, unmatched by anyone I've seen before or since. I used to tell friends that Michael was an alien, that he wasn't one of us. (I even once said that to Michael. He just giggled and said, "Oh, Ron, that's funny." I think he liked being called an alien.) His focus, his attention span, and his work ethic were far, far beyond that of an earthbound human being. He wanted to be the best, then go beyond that. It was always about making history, about moving the most units, about selling the most tickets, about making the most imaginative videos, about getting the most glowing reviews, and he was well aware that the only way to make that happen was to outwork, outstudy, and outthink anyone he perceived as a competitor. (The only other performer I've been around who comes close is Beyoncé. She's committed to her craft to the point of near-obsession. She's not quite an MJ-like alien, but it's close. As for the rest of the Jacksons, their main obsession was mostly money.)

Away from the studio, Michael Jackson was, to put it kindly, eccentric, in part because he lived in a world solely filled with music. He had a gift, but it was a *singular* gift, a gift that no one else in the world had, and he couldn't turn it off. (Elvis Presley was like that. He was so wrapped up in his life that he had to take something like forty pills to get his day started and forty-five more to wind it down.) On a daily basis, I told him to rest, to take a nap, to make sure he stayed healthy, but he *couldn't*. And unless you're around people like that—and very few of us are, because there are very few people like Michael Jackson—*you don't know*.

Part of it was that he had an addictive personality. But being addicted to making music is, for the most part, a positive thing. Being addicted to plastic surgery isn't. And that's something I tried to rein in. More than once, I told him, "Come on, Mike, cut that out. There's something wrong with this, man. You're a good-looking guy. You don't want to be white." I don't know how many times he had his nose done—at least a dozen—but it got so screwed up that no matter what the doctors did, it looked like it was going to fall off. Fortunately, his breathing wasn't affected by the surgeries . . . or at least not to the point that it shut him down.

Another addiction: Walt Disney. He knew everything there was to know about the Disney empire. There was something about the way Disney approached his art and business that was more than compelling to Michael—it was life-changing. I think part of what touched Michael was the familial aspect of what Disney had to offer; even though Michael came from a large family, he missed out on what a family was really about. (There were so many factions within the Jacksons and so much divisiveness that I can't imagine them sitting around the television watching *The Sorcerer's Apprentice*.) The Jacksons were far from the all-American family, and his father and his siblings all had their own agendas and aspirations. They were looking out for themselves—Michael, who wanted to be The Best, wasn't immune to that sort of single-mindedness—but all of that career-centricism didn't lend to a warm, nurturing environment. Disney movies, TV shows, toys, and clothes might have helped Michael fill some of those holes.

And he was *completely* obsessed with Disneyland. To celebrate its twenty-fifth anniversary in 1980, Michael was invited to perform there, but it wasn't just a single television special. We're talking six straight days at the Disneyland Hotel, and if you're like me, six straight days at Disneyland was as much fun as a hot poker up the ass. (Hell, two consecutive days was considerably more than enough.) Michael, however, was in heaven. He couldn't get enough. Each morning before we rehearsed, he went on as many rides as he could, the whole time screaming like he was a twelve-year-old. His favorite was the Space Mountain roller coaster, which he rode over and over and over again. He once dragged me on twice in a row, and he tried for a third, but I looked him straight in the eye and said, "Michael. Enough." For him, it was *never* enough.

As entranced as he was with the rides, he was also fascinated with the park employees who walked around in the hot sun wearing the Mickey Mouse and Pluto costumes. He badly wanted to speak with them, but Disney policy was such that they weren't allowed to remove their giant heads anywhere in public view, so the two of us hung out by their private changing area, waiting for their shift to end. After they removed their papier-mâché heads, Michael asked them what it felt like to walk around the park, and if they enjoyed working for Disney, and if they had any aspirations beyond being Donald Duck. The Disney-ites were flattered by all the attention and happily spilled their guts. Michael listened for hours. He couldn't get enough.

He liked to stay in the park after hours and watch the army that cleaned the park, then prepared it for the next day: the gardener who replaced the broken shrubbery, the painter who touched up the scraped bench, the guy with the huge ladder who replaced the burned-out street lights. This was fascinating to Michael, as it was a world of make-believe, and he was part of it.

All of Michael's hard work might have gone for naught, because Joe didn't care who he did business with as long as it put some money in his pocket, and that sort of thinking could've ended Michael's career before it even started, the kind of thinking that led to associations with people like Norby Walters.

Norby ran a club in New York called Norby Walters—he wasn't the most modest person in the world—which was funded by the mafia. Without asking me, Joe set up a meeting with me, Norby, and Norby's associate Michael Franzese, son of my old pal from the early Buddah days, Sonny Franzese. After about thirty seconds of pleasantries, Norby said, "We're promoting the next Jacksons tour."

I said, "Excuse me?"

"Yeah, we worked out a deal with Joe," Franzese said.

"But we need you to work out the black-and-white aspect of things," Norby said.

"Guys," I said, "we don't need to worry much about the black and white. The brothers are just concerned about the green. But I'm in control. Thanks for your offer."

Norby said, "We worked it out with Joe. We're gonna be your partners on this tour. The deal's in place. We'll give you a couple days to think about it, then we'll come back."

It was a threat—a subtle one, but a threat nonetheless—but I wasn't particularly concerned, because I'd been threatened hundreds of times by people far more frightening than those two . . . although Michael's father was a slight concern. Sure enough, two days later, they waltzed into my office, accompanied by an obvious mob goon. This time, there weren't any pleasantries.

Before they even sat down, I said, "I talked to the brothers, and this isn't gonna happen. Whatever you worked out with Joe, that's between you and Joe. But as far as the Jacksons and I are concerned, you guys are not a part of this tour."

And then the goon pulled a gun from his pocket and pointed it at my face.

And then I pulled a gun from the top drawer of my desk and pointed it at his face.

In the midst of our stare-down, Freddy DeMann ran into my office, looked at me, looked at the goon, looked at the guns, then turned right around and ran out. Fortunately, no triggers were pulled, and Norby, Franzese, and the goon left.

But here's what I didn't know: Across the street from my office, sitting in a nondescript car, were a couple of FBI agents. Turns out that the Feds had been keeping close tabs on Norby, who, along with his partner Lloyd Bloom,* was in the midst of a sports scandal, having landed professional contracts for college basketball players before they were eligible to play in the NBA. (There was also a bit of racketeering and extortion involved, but what's a bit of racketeering and extortion between friends?)

A couple months later, I was handed a federal subpoena, which said that I had to fly to Chicago so I could testify in Walters and Bloom's trial. I called my lawyer and said, "I don't want to fucking do this."

"You have to," he said. "If you don't, you'll be arrested."

"This is what I'm paying you $400 an hour for?"

"Yes. Your bill is in the mail," he said, then he hung up.

I immediately called my go-to security guy for the Jacksons tour, an LAPD officer named Clay. "I need you to look at the subpoena," I told him. "I'm messengering it over right now."

He called me a couple hours later and said, "Okay, this is what we need to do. We need to get you in and out of

---

* Not long after this all went down, Bloom was found dead in his car, killed by a bullet to the head.

Chicago as fast as humanly possible. You don't book anything yourself. You don't register at the hotel. Your name isn't to be mentioned anywhere. And I'm coming with you, and I'm bringing two of my guys."

I said, "Isn't that a little much?"

"Trust me," he said. "You need three guys. Because there's a problem."

"What kind of problem?"

"Don't worry about it. We're taking care of it."

"Do I need to bring a gun?" I asked.

"No. No guns. We've got that covered."

"Are you sure? I'd kind of like one."

"You can't get one on the plane. We can."

"Makes sense."

A few days later, without having told a single person the truth about where I was headed, I was on my way to Chicago, accompanied by three rather large armed men. After landing at O'Hare, we were met at the gate by a couple of scary-looking gentlemen in suits, who hustled us into an unmarked car. They took back roads and side streets to the hotel, where I was ushered into a side door, then led through the basement and up ten flights of stairs to my room. It turned out that the trial was all over the news, and the last thing that anyone wanted for me was to have my face plastered all over the print and electronic media. Especially me.

The next morning, we reversed the route, then took the unmarked car to the Dierksen Federal building, where we went through the same routine: basement door, back stairway, and so on. In the courtroom, after I was sworn in, I said, "Listen, I just want it on record that I didn't voluntarily come here to testify. When this goes public, I want everybody to know that I was subpoenaed."

The judge said, "Duly noted," and then he grilled me about how I met Norby and Michael and asked for specifics about our business dealings. I gave them the truth, the whole truth, and nothing but the truth, and then they sent me on my merry way.

We then made the mistake of going out the front door.

Now for my entire career—up until this book, as a matter of fact—I've made it a point to stay in the background, because my job isn't about me, it's about my clients. (There are plenty of other music managers who feel differently. It won't be too hard to name a few off the top of your head.) So it wasn't like the throng of media types were familiar with me . . . and that's just the way I wanted it to stay. As we headed back to our unmarked car, I didn't say shit to anyone.

Walters and Bloom negotiated a plea bargain, so my testimony didn't mean a thing. But a year later, Franzese and his crew were caught hijacking gasoline trucks.

Anyhow, in spite of the group's second wave of success, Michael wanted to stretch his wings, to try his hand in different media, so when the opportunity to star in the film *The Wiz* presented itself, he jumped. And thank goodness he did, because that was the beginning of his partnership with Quincy Jones, a partnership that changed the course of music history.

Adapted from the Broadway play of the same name, *The Wiz* was, for lack of a better description, the black version of *The Wizard of Oz*. The play, which ran for years and years,

Michael Jackson on *The Wiz* party train

was a huge success, and there was no reason to think the movie wouldn't follow suit. After all, it was going to star Michael, Diana Ross, Lena Horne, and Richard Pryor, plus the director was Sidney Lumet, and Quincy was the music supervisor. What could go wrong? The answer: everything. It lost over $10 million at the box office, and, unlike today, it couldn't make up for it with DVD and foreign sales.

But two good things came of the film: (a) It garnered a flock of Oscar nominations for the film's various art departments, and (b) that's where Michael met Quincy.

The View from Quincy Jones

I was a fan of Michael's since I saw the Jackson Five on *The Ed Sullivan Show* in 1969, but I never had the chance to get close to him. When I started working with him, the thing that knocked me out was his level of preparedness. He didn't just know his part in *The Wiz*, he knew everybody's, and not just their dialogue, but their songs and their dance steps. He would wake up every day at 5:00 a.m, and be on the set when filming started, whether or not he was needed on the set. He was that dedicated.

I remember the moment I decided I wanted to make a record with him someday. He was rehearsing with Sidney and the four principals, and, in one of his lines, he had to refer to Socrates, which he mispronounced as Sew-crates. The next day, same thing, and the day after that, and the day after that. Finally, I pulled him aside and said, "Michael, it's Sock-ruh-tees, not Sew-crates."

He looked me straight in the eye, like a deer in the headlights, and said, "Really?"

"Really. I promise you, man." Something about the way he said "Really" touched me. It showed me that he was inquisitive and ready to learn. It made me think, *someday, I'd like to make music with this boy.*

The film was shot at the old World's Fairgrounds in Flushing Meadows, New York, and the shoot seemed endless, although compared to how Hollywood films are made today, it was probably no time at all. During the shoot, there was a lot of downtime—making a movie involves a lot of stopping and starting, and hurrying up and waiting—which meant Michael and his co-stars had plenty of time to chat. He was friendly with Diana from their Motown days,* and, at that point, wanting to learn everything he possibly could about every aspect of the music industry in preparation for his inevitable solo career, he spent his spare hours grilling her. He was also well aware of Quincy's history, so the two of them talked and talked, ultimately learning that they had more in common than either could've imagined, both personally and musically. Quincy was the teacher, and Michael was the more-than-willing student. Michael earned his master's degree in music business on the set of *The Wiz* from two of the finest professors he could hope for. Plus Quincy was—and is—a nice person. He'll engage with anyone . . . even me.

Quincy and I became tight during the shoot. I knew and respected his work—hell, anyone in the music industry with even one ear respected what Quincy had done—and the chance to get such quality time with a man of his caliber was a thrill. He was the consummate music guy, always full of interesting ideas, always willing to share his ideas with anyone who'd listen . . . and if you had a suggestion that would improve one of his ideas, he'd take it to heart; the man had no ego, and his only concern was writing, arranging, or producing the best song possible. If someone said to him, "Hey, Q, how about adding some horns and strings during the last time through the chorus," he'd either say, "That's a terrific idea," or "Convince me why you think that's a good idea." He rarely, if ever, dismissed something out of

---

* Even though Diana didn't actually discover him. You're welcome, Gladys!

Quincy Jones and me at Quincy's house

hand, and there aren't too many people out there at his level who are that eager to collaborate.

The first and greatest lesson I learned from Quincy was to question anyone who told you that you couldn't do something. Roadblocks don't thwart him, they motivate him. Even today, he embraces the challenge of proving the naysayers wrong. "Music is an art form," he once told me. "It's a challenge, because unlike most every other art form, you can't do it alone. Compromise isn't a bad word. If you have the opportunity to collaborate with somebody, there's always the chance that they can take what you do and raise it to the next level. And always look to work with the best people possible, because they're going to make you look better. Also, you have to get people to believe in you, and that means musicians, record label employees, the money guys, *everybody*, because in our business, nobody, but *nobody* can do it alone. And don't be afraid to try *everything*. Make sure you get up to bat. If you strike out, you strike out, but at least you got in a few swings, and swings are important, because one of those swings might turn into a hit." See? The finest professor Michael, I, or anyone could hope for.

I don't know if Quincy out and out told Michael to go solo, but after they were done shooting *The Wiz*, Michael was ready to move on. He even had a game plan of sorts, which included having Quincy as part of his team, something that would soon bite us in the ass.

When Michael announced to his brothers that he was leaving the group so he could do his own thing, Randy, Jackie, Marlon, and Tito were beyond pissed, because Michael was their meal ticket. Promoters weren't interested in the group without Michael, and the brothers knew it. The issue for Michael was that he loathed confrontation. He couldn't deal with problems, he couldn't say no, he didn't want to get dirty. Conflict wasn't part of the bright, clean, shiny world he wanted to create for himself.

Which meant that I had to play the heavy. I had to be the guy to tell the brothers that Michael was going to make his own record, and the Jacksons were going to be his second priority. "It's not that he doesn't care about you guys as people or bandmates," I explained. "He just wants to do his own thing. It's not personal. It's about making music."

This was a difficult position for me to be in, especially when it came to Joe. In typical Joe fashion, he was acting paranoid, believing that Quincy and I were in cahoots, trying to steal Michael away from him. The brothers, to some extent, agreed with Joe, because on a certain level, they couldn't believe that Michael would make a decision like this of his own volition. There had to be external forces at work, and those external forces were named Quincy Jones and Ron Weisner.

I didn't relate the specific details of the meeting to Michael. The less he knew, the better. But I will say that I could tell he was thrilled the deed was done, and he didn't have to do it himself

Those meetings, as was the case with practically every business-oriented post-*Destiny* get-together with Joe and the brothers, were surreal. They were almost always held at the Hayvenhurst Estate in Encino, the estate in which most of them lived. I was usually able to tell how the meetings were going to go as soon as I stepped through the door. If the brothers were all wearing sunglasses, or if Joe was grunting rather than talking, it wasn't going to be an enjoyable afternoon. (Then again, if Joe was talking rather than grunting, it was also pretty bad.) Those chats usually involved lots of cursing, finger pointing, and accusations, especially from Joe: "Who's running this family? What do you know about taking care of my kids? They do what I tell them to do! You can't tell them what to do and get away with it, because I can have you disappeared in a minute! You Jews are just out for yourselves! You just want to get yours!"

Inevitably, Michael was nowhere to be seen.

I wasn't the only one to suffer the brunt of Joe's wrath. The agency that handled the Jacksons' concert bookings was called Triad Artists. The head of the agency was a guy named Richard Rosenberg, and Peter Grosslight was the Jacksons' day-to-day contact man. One afternoon in the midst of all the Michael-is-leaving crap, the three of us were summoned to Hayvenhurst for a meeting with Joe. When we arrived at the house, we pulled up to the front gate, buzzed the doorbell, then the gate opened, and we drove in. The second we got out of the car, Joe, the motherfucker that he was, released his two angry German shepherds. He called them off before they took a bite out of one of us. What a guy.

We finally made it into the house and into the living room. When I saw the brothers all had on their sunglasses— Michael included—I whispered to Richard, "Get ready. This is gonna be a pain in the ass."

Man, was I right about that.

Joe had decided that he was going to make a last-ditch attempt to bring Michael back into the fold for another tour. "And I'm gonna be in control. I'm putting things back the way they should be. I'm hiring a black promoter named Leonard Rowe, not you white Jews. I trust Brother Leonard. You got that, *Rosenberg?* You got that, *Weisner?*" He laid into our names, as if to remind us that we were white Jews.

Joe Jackson could've talked about black power until he was blue in the face, but the fact of the matter was that he brought in Rowe—an obvious hustler—because the two of them had a side deal that put more money in both of their pockets. That was another one of Joe's scams-of-the-week. But that all paled in comparison to his network of black promoters across the country.

The proliferation of segregation in the music world, circa 1980, was a dirty little secret; it was most evident when it came to concert promotion. In a nutshell, black acts used black promoters, and white acts used white promoters. Sliminess knew no race: There was an equal percentage of underhanded businessmen of every color. Joe Jackson managed to find most every underhanded black promoter in the country—some of whom had never promoted a show in their lives—and made backdoor deals with almost all of them.

The deals were dependant on how the band's fee was structured. Sometimes the group received an up-front deposit (usually 50 percent), while in other instances—especially if we weren't too sure about the promoter—we'd either be paid in full before we even set foot in the venue, or the fee would be put into an escrow account. Joe's deals took different forms, but the most common scheme was that the promoter held back some of the ticket proceeds, kept some for himself, and gave a percentage to Joe. If you asked Joe about it, he'd justify it by saying, "My kids made the money." Of course they did—there was no way he could siphon off *everything*—but they made considerably less than they would have had Joe not been in the picture.*

Even before we started working with Joe, I had a gut feeling that there was something dirty going on, so I told Freddy, "I don't know exactly what Joe is up to, and I can tell the

* Eventually, Joe even got some white promoters to play along.

brothers about it, and maybe they'll believe me, and maybe they won't, but that's between them and their father. But no matter what, we need to make sure we get paid what we're entitled to, and we need to make sure that there's no way anyone could possibly think our hands are dirty. I don't want anyone's money coming to us, other than ours. I don't want promoters sending us the brothers' money, then we have to dole it out, because if the brothers do the math, they'll probably say that we're ripping them off, because I don't think they'd blame their father." We decided that when it came to concerts, we'd get paid directly from either the agent, the promoter, or our tour manager or tour accountant. When it came to royalties, we'd get paid directly from the label. This sort of payment structure wasn't unheard of, but it wasn't typical. It was a pain in the ass to get it put in our artist/manager contract, but in the end, it was well worth the hassle. (In contrast, with Gladys Knight, *everything* went through her accountant. I was so comfortable with her team that there were a couple of instances when she was on the road and, for whatever reason, the group was in a financial bind. The accountant would ask me if they could defer my payment for three months, and I'd say, "No problem," because I knew that if they said three months, they meant three months. There's no way I'd accept that from Joe Jackson because there's no way I'd ever see that "deferred" money.*)

Joe had the uncanny ability to attract bloodsuckers, people who wanted something for nothing. (This was a gift

---

* The only act I managed who stiffed me was the Isley Brothers. I found out that my old neighbors from 1650 Broadway—specifically Ronald Isley—were "creative" accountants, e.g., "One for you and six for me." He tried to pull that shit with the IRS and ended up getting imprisoned for tax evasion.

he passed on to his children, but it didn't manifest itself in them until later.) Another classic example of Joe gumming up the works: During the *Thriller* recording sessions, the receptionist poked her head into the studio and said, "Ron, there are a couple of Asian gentlemen here to see you."

"What do they want?"

"They said it was personal."

Mildly intrigued, I went out to meet my visitors. After we shook hands, the shorter of the two said, "We just had a meeting with Joe Jackson about a project, and . . ." I should've stopped them right there. But, out of morbid curiosity, I let them continue, ". . . he told us Michael would participate."

Because I'm a polite man, I didn't tell them to fuck off, but rather, "I'm afraid Joe was mistaken. I can assure you that Michael knows nothing about this. I'm sorry you've been misled."

"Joe told us Michael would be available for us, for . . . " He then went on to describe a television project that didn't have a network, a producer, or financial backing but was guaranteed to be a smash, and he'd only need Michael for a month, maybe two.

"That's absurd," I said.

"And we paid him twenty-five thousand dollars."

"That's idiotic."

Glaring, the taller gentleman said, "We have to call Joe Jackson."

"I don't know what *he's* gonna tell you, but *I'm* telling you that for the foreseeable future, Michael won't be taking on any more projects. He's over-committed as it is. I'm sorry if there's been a misunderstanding." They walked away pissed. And these kinds of things happened once a week. One time it would be a hulking man from Ethiopia, while others, it would be a barely dressed woman from Santa Monica, all looking for time, all complaining that they'd paid Joe. It inevitably led to yet another Weisner–Jackson World War . . . especially when he sent these moochers, hustlers, and con artists to the offices of Weisner/DeMann Entertainment.*

Massive confrontations between Joe and me were a weekly event. The best I could hope for was that we yelled at each other on the phone, rather than at the studio. When Michael was in a zone where he could make the magic, I wanted him to stay there, and Joe was an expert at rattling his sons. But the brothers never protested his machinations and intrusions, Michael included. Why? Because their father petrified them. He'd abused them their entire lives, and, at that point, they were still scared. Even though they were grown men, there were times when I doubted that the brothers could *ever* break Joe's hold. And this was one of them, and that was unfortunate, because, as I told them during a meeting the next day, if Rowe took over the tour, they wouldn't see all the money they'd been contractually promised. Ever.

And I was right. Here's the deal:

On your typical tour, a band has a tour manager who often acts as the group's accountant, and one of his jobs is to settle up with the promoter at the end of the night. Sometimes they're paid then and there, while other times

_____

* He couldn't even mourn his son without trying to sell something. The day of Michael's funeral, he held a press conference in which he announced the arrival of his new record label.

it's about signing and processing the proper paperwork. At the beginning of the tour in question, the Jacksons were playing the Oakland Coliseum. Right before the band was going to take the stage, our tour manager/accountant, whose name was, I kid you not, Rusty Hooker, burst into the dressing room, grabbed me by the arm, said, "Ron, we have a problem," then dragged me out into the hallway.

"What do you mean *we* have a problem?" I asked after I took my arm back.

"Actually, *you* have a problem, because you're the one who has to go in there and tell them we're not getting all of our money tonight."

"What're you talking about?" I think we were due $300,000.

"Joe took half up front, but I never heard. And I just found out about it. And I don't know where he is."

I shrugged and said, "Nothing I can do. It's out of my hands," then went into the dressing room to break the news. After a moment of charged silence, one of the brothers said, "If we ain't getting paid, we ain't going on." I thought, *Great, now they decide to make a stand against Joe.*

"Guys, you gotta go on. If you don't, there'll be a riot." The stadium was beyond sold out, and even from where we were situated, we could hear the fans stomping the metal bleachers.

Another brother said, "Then you'd better get in touch with Joseph. You'd better get our money."

I decided it was time to give them a dose of cold, hard reality. "He took your money, and you're not gonna get it back unless you fight for it."

Another brother said, "It's your job! You're our manager!"

I said, "He's *your* father. *You* deal with it."

After ten or so minutes of this, they went on, because they knew if they didn't, there was a chance they wouldn't get out of Oakland alive. I have no idea whether Joe gave them their $150,000. But I doubt it.

And then there was Joe's merch scam.

One of the most underappreciated income streams for your typical band is the merchandise, or merch, i.e., T-shirts, hats, programs, key chains, buttons, and the like. In order for you to sell your merch in any union venue, you have to pay a percentage to the building, usually around 20 percent. Before you get to see any of the money from your sales, the building takes their cut.

That's inside the building. No artist allows their official merch to be sold outside of the building for the simple reason that it's illegal. Any T-shirt you see outside of a concert is dirty, and I don't mean in the run-it-through-the-washing-machine sense. So if you're a cop and you need to make your arrest quota, wander around the area a block or two from the Staples Center after a Jay-Z show and bust anybody selling a bootleg baseball hat with a blinking light. Ch-ching.

We were on the Southern leg of the *Destiny* tour; in one week we were hitting Raleigh-Durham, Charlotte, and Atlanta. In Raleigh, when we pulled the bus into the venue's parking lot, I noticed a mangy-looking guy selling a Michael T-shirt, a nice, professional-looking one, a design I'd never seen before. But bootlegs are a regular part of my life, and I had enough battles to fight, so I let it go. A couple days later in Charlotte, same deal, we pulled into the lot, and there's the same shirt . . . and I could swear it was the same guy. But you see a lot of people, and a lot of T-shirts, and I was tired, so again, I let it go. A few days after that, Atlanta. It was sweltering inside the arena, so I stepped outside to get some fresh air. The parking lot was surrounded by a large fence, outside of which stood a bunch of people hawking bootleg Michael T-shirts. And was one of those people that guy from Charlotte and Raleigh?

I clicked on the walkie-talkie, called one of the security men, and told him to investigate. Ten minutes later, he called me back and told me to meet him on the other side of the building. When I arrived, he pointed to a truck parked right outside the main entrance. We watched as people removed full boxes of T-shirts out of the truck, while others returned with enormous wads in their pockets. You'd have to be a moron to not know what those wads were made of.

I told my security guy, "Go get a couple more of our guys, go out to the truck, and grab the shirts."

Twenty minutes later, the walkie-talkie came to life: My security man. "What's up?" I asked.

"Okay, I got the shirts, and I got the cash. But check this out: These guys say Joe knows about this."

"*What?!*"

"Yeah, after he gave me the stuff, he said, 'I don't know why you're getting uptight about this. The guy I'm working for has a deal with Jackson. He knows all about it.'"

Of course he did.

Joe made life difficult not just for me, and not just for the label, but for *everyone*. (I suspect some of his more nefarious business associates might disagree. But maybe not.) Part of his proprietariness stemmed from the fact that he felt had he not pushed Michael et al. so hard, they wouldn't have succeeded, so in his mind, his piece of the pie should have been as big, if not bigger, than everyone else's. Eventually, Joe and the brothers realized that Michael was going to do what Michael was going to do, and nothing they said would change their minds.

Thus began preparation for the album *Off the Wall.*

And thus began the next chapter of my life.

CHAPTER EIGHT

Michael

Do I think Michael Jackson was a normal person? Absolutely not.

Do I think he was a pedophile? No.

Do I think he had issues? No question.

Do I think he was an unhappy guy? In a lot of respects, yes.

Do I think he would've been happier if someone were looking out for him from the minute he left the Jackson Five until he died? Emphatically, yes.

Michael Jackson and I wanted to hire Quincy Jones to produce his first solo record, but the honchos at Epic Records balked, and this was baffling. Yes, Quincy was known as a jazz arranger and composer—understandable, as he's worked with everyone from Count Basie to Ella Fitzgerald to Cannonball Adderley—but he had pop, rock, and R&B chops to burn, as witnessed by his recordings with Ray Charles, Little Richard, and Billy Preston, not to mention the series of funky solo albums he cut for A&M Records. If you were an executive at a major record label, circa 1980, you should have known that. They should have realized that getting Quincy Jones to produce an album for you was a coup.

The View from Quincy Jones

Motown also said I was too jazzy. When Marvin Gaye told Berry Gordy, "I want to use Quincy on *What's Going On*," Berry said, "Too jazzy." They were acting like I was following the trends, but in reality, we were helping establish the trends. Besides, jazz musicians like Lionel Hampton and Louis Jordan invented rock music. Saying it was Bill Haley and Elvis Presley was bullshit. And you can quote me on that twenty times.

Michael came to me crying when he thought they weren't going to use me. I put my arm around him and said, "Michael, everything will be just fine. Trust me, man. Trust me."

But Epic felt that Quincy was too old for Michael, who, in their minds, was a bubblegum kid who needed a bubblegum producer. (I was half-worried they'd call Kasenetz and Katz.) They believed that Quincy was out of touch with what the young people were listening to, which was a misnomer, as born out by his 1978 album *Sounds . . . and Stuff Like That!*, which hit number 15 on the *Billboard* Top 200 . . . and you don't climb into the top 20 with an audience entirely composed of listeners above the age of thirty.

Michael was adamant that Quincy get the gig, which meant that *I* was adamant that Quincy get the gig, so we took a meeting with the label honchos, including the label's general manager, Don Dempsey, and their head of A&R, Larkin Arnold. The several times I tried to get them to offer us a specific reason why they were balking at Quincy, the

answer was almost always the same: "We just don't feel it."
They didn't understand that Michael had a vision for the
record, a belief that together, he and Quincy could create a
product that would transcend race, age, and genre; that's
not the kind of strategy that can be accomplished with a
flavor-of-the-month producer. We needed someone who had
experience, a global view, and a good relationship with
Michael. Quincy was all of the above.

Unsurprisingly, Joe Jackson made the situation worse.
For a variety of reasons, he also wanted nothing to do with
Quincy, the primary one being that Joe recognized Quincy
had become a surrogate father to Michael. Hell, *everyone*
recognized that, but you couldn't help but notice; I mean,
they'd grown so close to one another that it got to the point
where they finished each other's sentences. That's a spirit
you can't buy or manufacture. You can hire the hottest producer in the world, but if he doesn't mesh with the artist,
it won't work. Figuring there wasn't enough room for both
him and Quincy, Joe did everything he could think of to
keep Q off the project.

These discussions went on for a couple of months, and
what with all the personalities and egos involved, it often
became nasty. If I were Quincy, considering how shabbily
he was treated, I probably would've walked, but he wanted
the gig, and he was going to fight for it. Eventually, we
started playing hardball—the Jacksons' last album, *Destiny*, had sold a couple million copies, so we had a little
bit of leverage—threatening to leave the label. (I'm not 100
percent certain we could've gotten out of the contract, but
had we tried to, it would've kept Epic tied up in court for

who-knows-how-long.) Eventually, after a lot of kicking and screaming, Epic reluctantly acquiesced. I think part of the reason Epic gave Quincy the thumbs-up was the fact that he didn't take much money up front. Either that, or they were fed up with me yelling at them for three hours a day.

Once all the dust settled, and we dived into preproduction, everyone sensed that this was going to be something above and beyond your typical album, even the Epic naysayers. The way Michael and Quincy interacted whenever they discussed the music was electric. Sometimes you go into a project without a clue as to how it'll turn out, while others, you know it's going to be a disaster, while yet others, you'll think, *Hmm, this might be okay.* But rarely, if ever, can you sense that the music will *transcend*, and that was the case here. (That all said, there's absolutely no way to discern whether a song or an album will be a hit. If I could figure out that formula, the world would be a better place for us all.)

The sessions were a sight to behold, in that Michael and Quincy wanted everything to be *perfect,* from the reverb on the snare drum, to the EQ on the bass, to the treatment of the vocals. Their goal was to mix soul, R&B, rock, pop, and jazz, and for that to work—for it to attract a wide, wide mainstream audience—everything had to be on point, *everything.* For the last five-plus years, disco ruled the charts, but it was on its way out, so the time was right to fill the void, but we knew we only had one shot, so we had to get it just right.

Michael and Quincy insisted that none of the music be created on a computer. They were going to use only experienced musicians, and they got some damn good ones, among them George Duke, David Foster, Wah Wah Watson, Greg Phillinganes, and Larry Carlton. Quincy kept those guys on call throughout the entire recording process, because if they needed something tweaked, they wanted to do it right then and there, while the idea was still warm. Quincy did whatever it took.

In terms of how the labor was divided, Michael and Quincy didn't have any kind of game plan. If one of them had an idea, they might ask the other to help them out, or they might do it themselves. It was an ego-free collaboration; they followed whomever came up with the best direction. They did whatever was necessary to nail it, and they went as long as necessary; I can't tell you how many times I heard someone say, "Do it again." This album was their life. They got into a zone, and the two of them became one.

When he was in the studio, Quincy came off like the classy veteran he was, a laid-back leader who was a pleasure to be around. Michael, even though this was his first time as the creative heart of an album, was equally easy to work with, but in a distinctly different fashion. He wasn't laid-back like Quincy, but he was so focused, determined, and confident that I knew I wouldn't have to worry about him . . . which left me plenty of time to worry about everything else.

One of my jobs was to be the Michael Jackson Gatekeeper, to make sure neither of them was disturbed in a way that would knock them out of their groove. I told Michael, "I'll block the bullshit. You guys do what you have to do, and I'll do what I have to do." Joe Jackson was the cause of much of the bullshit, naturally. He'd come by the studio for no reason, or he'd call to complain about something, or he'd send one of his shady friends over to visit. And he had a lot of shady friends; he was an asshole magnet.

Another one of my vital tasks: chauffeur. Because Michael didn't drive, I picked him up at home and dropped him at the studio, after which I'd either stay and hang out for one, or two, or five, or fifteen hours, or go back to the office and try to focus on something other than the album . . . which, frankly, was difficult, because I knew that there were special things happening at Westlake Studios. I knew we were taking The Next Step, and the second it hit the street, it would be the new paradigm for pop music.

After they were happy with the tracks, Quincy and Michael mixed and mastered the entire album, at which point Quincy, in his infinite wisdom, said, "We're all too close to this record. Let's take some time away from it, come back in two weeks, and listen with some fresh ears. Everybody's gotta walk away." Two weeks later, they listened again and remixed practically the entire album, deadlines be damned. (I don't remember the specifics about how late they were in turning in the album, but, man, they were *late*.)

To me, that's more proof that Quincy Jones is a true artist, because any true artist—musician, painter, writer, fashion designer—will always question his or her art. True artists will wonder, *What if I'd played a C# instead of an F#*, or *Might cerulean have been a better choice than navy*, and maybe they'll answer those questions, and maybe they won't, but they'll always wonder how or if they could make their work *better*. But even if they question it, they'll know when they can call it done, and that's something Quincy brought to the table. Michael could tinker with a track for weeks, so he needed someone to tell him, *That's fine, let's move on to the next one.* (Even when "Rock With You" became a smash, Michael still complained to me about how many different directions he could've taken with the track. It was the number one record in the world, and he still wasn't happy with it. But that was Michael.)

Michael and Quincy had a specific creative direction, *very* specific, and that direction was to make music for *everyone.* Their thinking was, *If you like soul, R&B, rock, pop, disco, or jazz, this record will be for you.* (As someone who'd produced, composed, and arranged in almost every musical style of the twentieth century, Quincy gets the lion's share of the credit for this diversity. But there were few singers back then who could sound natural in each setting, and I can't think of anyone other than Michael who could remain true to themselves in such diverse settings.) The label was resistant to investing that much time, energy, and money into *Off the Wall,* because of that ceiling. I knew their thinking: *Why should I let those two nuts spend months in the studio and blow their budget all to hell, when all we're gonna do is sell 1.3 million albums, and considering how lousy the last two Jackson records did, it'll probably be half that.* And I understood that. Those kinds of results were all they knew, but change, as they say, was in the air. They were scared to step up, to be aggressive, to be innovative. They didn't comprehend the path we were forging.

I tried to be empathetic, but it was hard. Everyone at the label, from the A&R staff to the marketing and promotion department, had to deal with an avalanche of new releases. Every week, two, five, eleven, twenty more records would be released, and they'd have to deal with them. So when people like Michael Jackson (who was probably perceived as a has-been) and Quincy Jones (who, as far as the music industry was concerned, was a jazz musician) come along and want to shake things up, to spend some money, to try something unique, the support isn't going to be there. From top to bottom and everywhere in between, the label was more concerned with schedules and stability than they were with innovation and daring.

The Columbia Records brain trust was on our backs almost daily, hammering home the point that the album had to be mastered and delivered by the contractually agreed-upon date, regardless of what kind of shape the record was in. A song isn't properly mixed down! *Too bad. We have a schedule.* We haven't recorded the horn section yet! *Too bad. We have a schedule.* Michael's not happy with his vocals on a couple of tracks! *Too bad. We have a schedule.*

It was obvious to any rational thinking person who heard the early mixes that something different was going on, something interesting, something all-encompassing, something eminently salable. But rationality went out the window because of the schedules, the schedules, the goddamn schedules.

And then there were the endless budget meetings with Epic's president, Don Dempsey, and his staff of yes-men. Don, while a very nice guy, lacked vision. He couldn't see Michael's potential, and he didn't want to spend any more money than he did for his other black acts . . . and the money decisions were made before the record was even finished.

I'd leave Don's office with my head spinning, and my stomach in knots, then head up to the studio and tell Michael and Quincy, "We've got problems. These guys aren't even on the same planet, let alone the same ballpark." But we decided to do what any good team player would do: ignore the Suits. Michael and Quincy weren't going to deem the record done until it was *done*, and they had my full support.

Once the record was done, it was time to put together the full package, and that meant photo sessions, and photo sessions meant drama with Michael. No matter how the pictures came out, his first comment was always along the line of, "Can we lighten my skin tone?" To keep the peace, the art director tweaked the shots to make him look incrementally less black.

The first pass wasn't light enough for him. Nor was the second pass. Nor was the third.

Looking at the fourth version of the photo, I said, "Michael, you're not white. We're not going any lighter. Accept it." And he did. But not the next time around.

All he said as he looked at the proofs from the *Thriller* photo session a few years later was, "Lighter, lighter, lighter, lighter."

I told him, "Michael, you can't go lighter. This isn't you. You have to stop. You can't be something you're not. People are going to laugh. You'll never hear the end of it." I briefly—*very* briefly—thought about going to his brothers for some advice but realized that they wouldn't help out because it didn't affect them. His sister Janet might have had something to say, but, at that point, she had her own problems—if I recall correctly, this was around the time she first took up with her future ex-husband and crackhead singer El Debarge—so she was out of the loop. And Joe? Forget it. The Jacksons were America's most dysfunctional family, so it was all on me.

I wasn't the only person who felt this way. Everyone at Epic Records was telling him the exact same thing. The art director called me several times and said, "Are you guys crazy? He's not a white guy." And Larry Stessel, their head of marketing, told Michael in no uncertain terms that lightening the skin tone was a horrible, horrible idea. "The press will chastise you," Larry told Michael. "And so will the black community."

After that meeting, Michael told me, "Call Walter Yetinkoff and get Larry fired."

The View from Larry Stessel

When I first met Ron, I was vice president of marketing, West Coast, for Epic Records. I became responsible for Michael's marketing on the tail end of *Off the Wall*. As ex–New Yorkers, Ron and I hit it off immediately. He was much more well-rounded than a lot of people in his position. He had a clear and distinct understanding of not only the music industry but of consumer buying habits and what consumers were looking for. He understood all aspects of the business, from promotion, to sales, to marketing, to advertising, and he had the right contacts when it came to the burgeoning business of video.

We knew video would be key for Michael, because he'd always been a TV star. From his appearances on *The Ed Sullivan Show* with the Jackson Five, to their Saturday morning cartoon, he was always the group's focal point. He knew how to work a camera and play to the audience, so when it came to making videos with prerecorded music, he knew how to make it look good.

Ron was very proactive and aggressive in introducing me to Michael. Michael always listened to what Ron had to say, and Ron spoke well of me, so my relationship with Michael was welcoming from the start . . . and he didn't welcome people very easily.

One weekend, I broke my ankle playing softball but couldn't take any time off work, because that Monday, I had to go to the recording studio so I could show Michael a two-page ad we were going to run in *Billboard* magazine, congratulating him on selling five million copies of *Off the Wall*. While I was still under the influence of pain medication, I pulled Michael aside to show him the ad. The photo in the ad was taken from a photo session in which the lights were quite hot, so hot that in the picture, you could see the beads of sweat on Michael's forehead. Our art director airbrushed them out, so in the shot, Michael's forehead looked perfectly clean and unblemished.

Michael glanced at it, then said, "You airbrushed the picture. I don't like my photos being retouched."

I said, "Well, it was hot, and you were sweating under the lights, and the designers felt you needed to be cleaned up a bit."

He said, "Don't ever retouch my photographs."

"Okay, no problem, we'll go back to the original one."

I didn't think anything of that conversation until I got a call from one of my superiors. "What did you say to Michael?" he roared. "Because he called Walter and told him that you called him dirty, smelly, and stinky." After I told him the story about the retouching discussion, he said, "Listen, just stay away from the project for a while. Let somebody else in your department meet with him, but you keep doing the work."

Several months later, I was at Ron's office. While we were looking at some photo proofs, Ron looked over my shoulder and said, "Hi, Mike. You remember Larry from the label, right?"

"Of course I do. Hi, Larry," he said, then gave me a huge hug. From that moment on, Michael and I were completely friendly, and I'm sure that was all because at some point, Ron told him to get over it.

I've never met anybody who doesn't like Ron. He's always been honest and fair, and I've never heard anybody say he cheated them, or he didn't live up to their promise, and in my business, that's really rare. He proved you can do it right without being an asshole.

Walter was the head of Columbia, and complaining to him would've been going Defcon 5. I thought, *Great, now he decides to get confrontational.* "Mike," I said, trying to keep my voice at a reasonable volume, "first of all, no matter how many records you sell, you can't alienate the label. You don't do that. The guy is taking care of business for us. If you cause trouble with Walter—not to mention going behind Larry's back—they'll bury you. And second of all,

Larry is one of our biggest supporters. He's always treated us right. You can trust him, and you can't say that about a whole lot of people."

"Well, maybe I'll call Walter myself."

"Please don't, Mike. *Please.*"

He didn't say he wouldn't make the call, but after thinking about it for a few days, I did indeed speak with Walter, not to complain, but rather to warn. "Listen, Walter, you might get a call in the next few days from Michael. He's going to want to discuss the cover shot for the album." I explained the shading situation, then said, "No matter how much he bitches about it, just say no."

"Am I gonna get pushed into a corner?" Walter asked. "Because I don't want to get pushed into a corner."

"Walter, if you get pushed into a corner, push back and get the hell out of that corner."

Michael never reached out to Walter, and thank goodness. The upshot was the cover shots were somewhat lightened, but he didn't look nearly as white as he'd look down the line. But later in life, it wasn't the photos that altered: It was him. And that broke my heart. He was a good-looking young man who became an odd-looking adult, and it was all his own doing.

Even before the album cover was approved, we were laying the marketing groundwork. Our smartest decision was servicing the advance copies of the album to more than one radio format. Instead of just hitting up black radio, we went everywhere, because that record had something for everyone. This wasn't a common approach to promotion; for the most part, labels were conservative about when, where, and how they spent their money. If we're talking about an urban act, you'd advertise in urban periodicals, period; and then if the record seemed poised to take the next step, you'd cast a wider net. (The record industry is one of the most reactive entities you'll ever find.) Such multitiered promotion wasn't unheard of, but it wasn't at all common, as there were only a small handful of acts that attracted such a mixed-race audience. Very few black artists crossed over to white radio, and very few white artists crossed over to black radio, and if it happened in either direction, it was a *long* process. But the 1979 version of Michael Jackson was one of the minority who appealed to everyone. (This seems unthinkable today, what with black artists ranging from Beyoncé to Drake to Lil Wayne popping up on radio and television outlets of all shapes, sizes, and formats.)

The Columbia and Epic brass wasn't eager to spend any extra money on promotion and marketing . . . until they heard the album—then they got it and started being helpful. Nonetheless, I was always budget conscious, because if you spend money willy-nilly, eventually you're going to spend it badly, whereas if you take your time and assess how an artist's album will fly with any given radio, television, or print outlet, and choose wisely, you'll be more efficient, and you won't piss off the record label numbers people. And, as has been noted, and as will be noted again, you never want to piss off anyone at the record label. Especially the numbers people.

One way we saved money, at least until we broke the bank for the "Thriller" clip, was by being smart with our video production. Up until director John Landis paired

Michael with a bunch of zombies, we were extremely conscious about our video budget, because we weren't looking
to make *The Empire Strikes Back*. All we wanted was a good
clip that (a) was representative of the music, and (b) the
fans would be willing to watch over and over again.

At this point, it's worth discussing music on television,
and Music Television.

Back in my Buddah days, music fans had few outlets to
see their favorite bands. They could *hear* them anytime they
wanted to, but viewing them was a rarity. Concert tours
were shorter, and bands hardly ever played at the secondary
or tertiary markets—such as Des Moines, Fargo, San Anto-
nio, and so on—and because there were only three major
networks, and because the three major networks wanted
to appeal to the largest cross section of viewers possible,
there was far more emphasis placed on family fare than on
rock 'n' roll, soul, or R&B.

Come the late 1960s and early 1970s, my colleagues
at the label and I felt that that was a crime. To us, music
on television was unchartered territory that needed to be
explored, and explored *hard*, because listeners had no way
to find out how their favorite artists moved or spoke, and the
only visuals came from album covers or magazine articles.
(To that end, when I was a kid, I loved listening to a nighttime radio deejay named Jack Lacey, who played all kinds
of great music on WINS-AM in New York. He had a deep,
booming voice, and I pictured him to be a six-foot-tall, six-
foot-wide hipster with a beret and a goatee. Several years
later, I was delivering some records to the music director at
WINS. We met in the lobby, where they were piping in what

was going out on the air. And then I heard *that* voice: It was Jack, filling in for one of the afternoon jocks. As we headed up the hallway leading to the music director's office, we ran into this short, scrawny, older, slightly stooped-over, plain-looking guy. Sure enough, it was Jack. My mind was blown.) We envisioned singers and bands on the tube as a new paradigm, a different, vital way in which to present (and sell) our artists.

And we were right. Soon enough, music crept its way onto TV and into living rooms. *American Bandstand* had been on since 1952, but in 1971, it was joined by *Soul Train*, then in '73, *The Midnight Special* and *Don Kirshner's Rock Concert*, and if you were a rock or R&B fan, you were in heaven. The shows were well produced and utilized the available sound and video technology to the fullest, and a quick YouTube search will show that these performances hold up wonderfully. You could finally see that the Doobie Brothers weren't actually brothers, and that Leon Redbone was an honest-to-goodness Native American who performed wearing traditional clothing, and that Marvin Gaye still had some great dance moves.

Even in those early days, despite the fact that it wasn't omnipresent, music on television became as important—if not more important—than music on the radio. Fans realized early on that the visual aspect enhanced the experience. And while that may seem obvious now, it wasn't then. Until that moment, radio had been enough. Putting a face and motion to the sound added a layer of intrigue that led not just to higher sales but also to greater loyalty and more interest in attending live shows.

This was impressive, considering the limited number of channels and time slots . . . but it could've been better. There was room for more. I knew that sometime, somewhere, someone would come up with something that would give me and my managerial brethren a vehicle to visually promote our artists. And I knew that when this entity found its footing, I could use it in a manner unlike anyone else.

Enter cable television. Enter MTV.

Like many groundbreaking television endeavors, the channel didn't get off to a terrific start when they launched in 1980. There weren't many videos, as record labels didn't initially believe it was worth spending the money on something they believed had little chance of amping up sales. The production values on the videos, while better than public access television, weren't anything to write home about. And the station's formatting, such as it was, didn't offer much of a sense of logic. They had some work to do.

But there was something there. And as I watched them iron out the wrinkles, it dawned on me that the majority of the clips on the station were, at best, simple, and, at worst, lacking any sense of artfulness whatsoever. The public, however, didn't have a basis of comparison—remember, to that point, the primary sources for music on television were *American Bandstand, Soul Train, Saturday Night Live, Rock Concert,* and *Midnight Special,* but those shows were only on once a week, plus *SNL* was only on seven or so months out of the year, plus three out of those five were on too late for many young kids to watch, and young kids buy a *lot* of records. The early videos that filled up MTV's daily programming schedule were, on a certain level, disposable novelties. None of them were live performances—we're talking all lip synching to a track, all the time—but music fans stuck with them, no matter how cheesy or low-rent they might have been, because there wasn't anything else out there. There was little, if anything, in the way of cinematic storytelling.

I'm not going to claim that Michael's videos from *Off the Wall* were all that different from the rest of the MTV fare. "Don't Stop 'til You Get Enough," for instance, while certainly entertaining, was certainly far from groundbreaking, although the bit where there were three MJs dancing in unison was certainly memorable. But it was entertaining, and it gave us a great jumping-off point . . . and, much to Epic's eternal pleasure, it was cheap. (Later on down the line, for instance, I hired Bob Giraldi to direct the video for "Beat It" off the strength of his work on some public service announcements for the Detroit Free Clinic. Even later on down the line, you had to spend money on videos in order to compete with everyone else who was spending money on videos. I hired a young commercial director by the name of David Fincher—you might've heard of him—to direct a couple of Steve Winwood's videos, and Dominic Sena of *Gone in 60 Seconds* fame to helm a piece for Robbie Nevil's "C'est La Vie." But Giraldi, Fincher, and Sena all understood what we were trying to do—be different, be meaningful.)

It's bizarre to consider this now, but when his videos premiered on MTV in 1980, the channel wasn't showing any clips from black artists. It wasn't because they were a racist organization, but rather because labels weren't shelling out the dollars to make videos for their black acts. I doubt there was any trepidation on MTV's part when "Rock with You" and "Don't Stop 'til You Get Enough" showed up at their doorstep—there likely weren't any meetings among their top brass in which someone said, "Guys, I don't know if this black thing is or isn't gonna work, but we're gonna have to try it eventually, and we've got this Jackson thing, so let's give it a shot"—but it was an issue nonetheless . . . that is, until the videos aired, and they were an immediate, massive success.

MTV wasn't the only television outlet that helped us. I landed Michael an interview with Sylvia Chase from ABC's *20/20*. She spent a week on the road with us, and on day one, Michael proved to be his own best PR person. The first show her crew covered was at the Oakland Coliseum, and to get into the stage area, the artist had to drive his vehicle down a long driveway, a driveway that was surrounded with barricades to keep the fans from attacking the car. As the driver of our stretch limo inched toward the drive-way, Michael looked at the throngs of people, and told the *20/20* producer, "Here's what's going to happen: I'm going to open the sunroof, and I'm going to climb out of the car and onto the roof and wave to the crowd, and you're going to film it." The producer seemed skeptical, but Michael assured her, "Trust me. It'll make a great shot."

The second our security guy heard that, he grabbed my elbow, pulled me close, and whispered into my ear, "Ron, Ron, don't let him do that. I think that's a horrible, horrible idea."

I said, "No shit," envisioning a riot that would be seen by millions of ABC's viewers, a riot that would make us look like unprofessional buffoons. But before either of us could stop him, Michael popped the roof, and the second the top of his afro saw the light of day, the fans went nuts. After about thirty seconds of madness, I grabbed Michael's wrist and yanked him back into the car, possibly harder than I should have. (I didn't hear the end of that for months.) The fans didn't riot, thank goodness, but they made a hell of a mess. It wasn't tragic by any means, but the cleanup crew at the Coliseum, well, suffice it to say they were more than a little pissed. But Michael craved that attention, and early in his career, that insatiable desire for the general public's love and adoration sometimes trumped logic, reason, or rationality.

Two weeks later, the head of security at the Coliseum called and asked, "What the hell happened there with you guys? Your boy almost caused a riot."

Music Manager Tip #1,562: When you get stuck in a pile of your own bullshit, deflect the blame. I said, "*Our* boy almost caused a riot? I don't know, it looked like some shitty security on your end."

But I digress. Yet again.

Off the Wall had been out for a couple of months when we began our tour. Michael had spent years on the road, and we were well familiar with the ins and outs of touring, but this was his first time going solo, and, in typical Michael fashion, he wanted it to be perfect, to give ticket buyers their money's worth, to deliver a whimsical night of entertainment, to elicit an even better reaction than that of the best Jackson Five shows. We built a backing band from some of the finest studio musicians in the world, and, at

Michael's insistence, brought in magician Doug Henning to help stage the shows.

During the initial planning meetings, Michael—along with our production manager, Chris Lamb, and Doug— listened patiently as Michael outlined his plans for the show, plans that included flying, and disappearing, and animals, and, of course, magic. I could tell by the thoughtful, somewhat confused expression on his face that Doug was trying to figure out how best to implement Michael's ideas, but before he could even answer, Chris and I started in with the logical questions: "How much equipment will we need? How long will it take to set up and break down the set? How much will it cost? Will we be able to haul it from city to city?" Much to Michael and Doug's chagrin, we weren't able to bring most of their staging ideas to life. Besides, if we had, it would've looked more like a circus than a concert. Once again, I had to play the heavy, to tell Michael what could and couldn't be done. Fortunately, Michael took a big picture view and didn't complain about the final concert product.

As noted, Michael was afraid to fly, so the entire circus traveled across the country on a bus. (To give you some perspective, the vast majority of superstars fly from city to city, while the sidemen and the crew are stuck on the bus.) Because I was part of the circus, I was on the bus too, and that drove me nuts. The confines were cramped, there was next to nothing to do, and this being 1980, there were no cell phones, so I wasn't able to get much work done. The highlight of travel days was when we pulled up at the truck stops on the side of the highway. The lowlight was every second

Michael Jackson test photograph of prototype iridescent tuxedo for *Off The Wall* project. It didn't work.

that Joe Jackson was on the bus, because no one wanted to deal with Joe, and because he felt bored and excluded, he'd break my chops, probably just to pass the time.

Traveling with just Michael was a much simpler, much more enjoyable endeavor, especially early in the game. Michael and I were in Europe promoting *Off the Wall* and were scheduled to do a few TV shows in England. As noted, Michael was a *hard* worker and took on every publicity opportunity, and I had to attend all of them, and it was exhausting. After a dinner on a rare night off, I went back up to my hotel room and, without even taking off my clothes, collapsed onto the bed. Right as I drifted off, the phone rang. Michael: "Ron, be in the lobby in ten minutes."

"What're you talking about, Mike? We're done for the day. We don't have anything else lined up."

"Just come down to the lobby. Ten minutes. Ya gotta come down."

I thought, *I gave at the office. I'm done for the day.* But Michael had a way of getting you to do what he wanted, so ten minutes later, I was down in the lobby, along with two of our security guys. I asked one of them where we were going. "I don't know," he said. "Mike just wants to go."

Two minutes later, we were in the car, on our way to the London Palladium, where we were to take in a performance by Liberace. I asked Michael, "Why are you making me do this?"

"You'll love it, Ron."

I thought, *No. No I won't.*

He continued, "And wait'll you see the opening act: The Dancing Waters. The water shoots up, and there are colors, and it's wonderful."

The Dancing Waters wasn't wonderful. This was the early days of computerized shows, and it was pretty crude. But Michael loved it. After the water went down the drain, the lights dimmed, and this overweight gay gentleman took to the stage, wearing a full mink coat. When he sat down at the piano, Michael clapped loud, long, and hard.

About twenty minutes into the show, I turned to one of our security guys and said, "This is it, man. I'm outta here. I can't do this." I left without saying goodbye to Michael, but he was so wrapped up in the show that he probably wouldn't have noticed anyhow.

The next morning, Michael called me in my room. *"Why did you go?!* The show was amazing! We spent an hour and a half in his dressing room, and you missed it!" I'd rarely heard him so pissed, and there was a brief moment when I thought he was going to (a) fire me, and (b) have one of our security guys take me out back. The moral of that story was, if Michael Jackson drags you to a concert, you stay until the bitter end, whether it's Liberace or James Brown.

All of that reminded me of the late-night phone call I'd received from him back in 1978: "Ron, wake up, Fred's coming to town!"

"Fred? Who's Fred?"

"Fred. *Fred.*"

"Fred who, Mike?"

"Fred Astaire! The American National Theater is giving Fred Astaire an award! The ceremony is at the Century Plaza Hotel! I gotta go. I gotta be in front!"

I bought us a table right in front of the stage, a stage that was about four feet off the ground. On each side of the stage sat an easel holding a 20' x 20' photo of Astaire with his top hat and cane. The whole night, Michael had a huge smile on his face, as if he was a nine-year-old gawking at a department store Santa. At the end of the night, when we stood up to leave, Michael said, "We can't go yet. We can't go until we get one of those."

"One of what?" I asked.

He pointed at the massive photo stage left. "One of *those*."

"Mike," I said, "I can't just go up there and take one."

He peered around the ballroom. "Nobody's looking. Grab it now!"

He was right. Nobody was looking. So I grabbed it. But I felt like a schmuck as I held it while we waited for the valet to return with my car.

Later that week in London, Michael and I were relaxing in his room, watching *The Top of the Pops*. I looked at it as the English version of *American Bandstand*, in that the show's live performers lip-synched their hits. Halfway through the show, the host—I think it was Simon Bates—said, "Ladies and gentlemen, Adam Ant!"

Michael and I knew of Adam, but we had yet to see him perform. He sounded great, but, more important for Michael, his look was arresting: He was clad in full military gear. Michael stared at the screen, silently, intensely. I could see the wheels spinning, but I wasn't sure in which direction.

The next day, in the midst of a press junket, Michael pulled me aside and said, "Ron, I have to find a costuming place."

I was used to Michael's often incongruous requests, but I still had to ask, "Why, Mike? Why do you need a costuming place?"

He grinned and said, "Adam Ant."

I asked around, and found out about Berman's and Nathan's Costumes of London, one of England's biggest wardrobing houses. They've provided costumes for dozens of war movies and period pieces, including *All Quiet on the Western Front, The Three Musketeers,* and *Empire of the Sun,* so they had everything. The following afternoon, a local costume designer and I scoured Berman's and Nathan's for a military outfit similar to Adam's. I picked out about twenty, then gave them to the designer and said, "Duplicate these."

For the rest of his life, Michael was rarely seen in public wearing anything other than a military uniform. And for that, you can thank Adam Ant. (P.S. Michael never credited Adam. Whenever he was asked about his obsession with military garb in an interview, he'd say, "I was inspired." That's all. Just, "I was inspired.")

That was the case with the moonwalk. Fans and media attributed the dance to Michael, but, as was the case with the military gear, it was something that he co-opted from another artist, and made it his own.

Michael Peters was one of Michael's first choreographers. Talented and a great guy, Peters, along with a gentleman named Lester Wilson, was the dominant force behind Michael's dancing. But he also got some help from a couple of underground break-dancers, Shabba-Doo and Dane Parker. Shabba and Dane had all kinds of new moves, but

Michael Jackson

Michael being Michael, he took these moves to a different place. He practiced, and practiced, and practiced some more, so by the time the world saw it for the first time on the *Motown 25* television special, it was his own and it was brilliant.

But I know why he didn't give Adam and the dancers their public due: He wanted everything he did to be something that hadn't been done before, and that included his opening acts. His litany was, "Find somebody that nobody's seen!" That was difficult, if not impossible, because in that day and age, anyone worth seeing had already been seen. So, as was often the case when it came to Michael, I had to think *way* outside of the box.

While scouring some entertainment trade magazine or another, I came across an ad for a guy who dubbed himself The Human Cannonball. He was an Italian nut who—you guessed it—had himself shot out of a cannon. That sounded right up Michael's alley, so I reached out to his people and had them send me a videocassette. When the cassette arrived the following week, it was accompanied with a note from The Cannonball himself: "I'm only able to do one show daily."

Of course you are, I thought as I put the tape into my VHS. I hit play and was treated to the sight of a slightly overweight middle-aged man being ejected from a cannon time and time again. Each time he got out of the landing net, he wobbled so much that I was certain if he fell, he wouldn't get back up again. It wasn't the most polished act I'd ever seen, but I showed Michael the tape anyhow.

Naturally, he loved it.

"I don't know, Mike," I told him, wishing I hadn't played the tape in the first place. "I'm not feeling this. It's like a sideshow." The second that left my mouth, I realized it was just about the worst thing I could say, because Michael *loved* circuses. But wiser heads prevailed, and Michael and The Human Cannonball thankfully never shared the stage.

The *Off the Wall* train never slowed; the record sold and sold and sold, but we didn't want to rest on our laurels. Back then, back in the early 1980s—which, considering the changes the music industry has undergone seems like a century ago—you couldn't wait four years between new pieces of product. Once you'd mined your album for its singles, and once you'd toured the world three or four times, you had to get your ass back into the studio and start again. You couldn't disappoint your loyal fans, because they didn't have the Web, or iTunes, or smart phones to keep them entertained—they had you, and if you weren't there, they'd be less than pleased. It wasn't so much *out of sight, out of mind*, as it was *out of sight, where did you go?*

By the time he started recording the album *Thriller* in the spring of 1982, I was with Michael every day. We almost always met at his house, because (a) I lived just a few blocks away, and (b) as I mentioned earlier, he couldn't drive. Then we'd head over to the studio, where he'd spend hours upon hours working on bits and pieces of tunes that, more often than not, never saw the light of day. After ten, or twelve, or fifteen hours in the studio, we hopped into my car—which, what with its state-of-the-art sound system was a rolling studio—and listened to the cassette tapes featuring the fruits of his labor. More often than not, while checking out a sliver of music he'd worked on for three hours, he'd say, "I'm not happy," and then, the following day, start from scratch. Very few people had the opportunity to witness his perfectionist tendencies. There's a reason why, for a while, he was the greatest entertainer in the world. You have to work for it. And Michael Jackson worked his ass off.

(Side note: Generally, Quincy was fine with this sort of obsessiveness—for that matter, unlike few others, he was often able to guide Michael into a better place. But sometimes, Michael had an idea that he wouldn't let go, and he'd dig in his heels. Quincy is the master—or should I say The Master, with capital letters—yet he had no ego. He'd use whatever worked . . . or, in some instances, whatever made his artist happy.)

(Another side note: Sometimes, Michael arrived to the studio hauling a big burlap bag, which he'd throw onto the mixing console. In the bag: his big-ass snake, Muscles. When Quincy or the engineer tried to move the reptile, he hissed like a madman. Quincy indulged Michael's quirks—he believed that personal idiosyncrasies could lead to brilliant music—but the engineers, not so much. One of them would say, "goddamn snake," and then Michael went nuts, not because they were insulting his pet, but rather because they were cursing. See, you couldn't swear around Michael; it drove him crazy. And god knows he never cursed. If he had to go to the bathroom, he wouldn't say, "I have to take a piss," but rather, "I have to go tinkle." And if somebody dropped an F-bomb, forget it. He'd cover his ears, close his eyes, and whisper, "Don't say that don't say that don't say that don't say that.")

As was the case on *Off the Wall,* Michael worked hard, but he worked in a positive manner. Even when there were creative clashes, most every day at the studio was a joy. And the guests that stopped by to work inevitably brought great energy and exuberance. Everyone was united in a singular goal: to make the best record possible. Paul McCartney was no exception.

Michael had known Paul for years, and during the *Thriller* preproduction meetings, he suggested that inviting Paul to sing on a song would be yet another way to make this album stand out. It took some convincing—numerous phone calls from Michael, Quincy, and me over the span of several weeks, specifically—but he finally agreed. When Paul ultimately made it to the studio, he and Michael had a great time together, and, as is always the case, Paul brought a level of enthusiasm and professionalism that was a breath of fresh air. To me, "The Girl is Mine" is the weakest track on the album, but Paul's appearance was one of the highlights of the recording process.

Michael spent a lot of time grilling Paul about how he built his publishing catalog. Paul, an easygoing guy, answered every question patiently and in great detail, not knowing that three years later, Michael would buy the Beatles catalog right out from under him. Paul felt betrayed by the way Michael's team handled the transaction, and the two didn't speak until 1989, when I got them together while I was managing McCartney. They made their peace, but it was an uneasy one.

Even though *Off the Wall* and *Thriller* were different animals musically speaking, the creative and recording

Michael Jackson and Paul McCartney. Only photo of "The Girl is Mine" recording session.

Rehearsal for Paul McCartney tour. Paul McCartney and Ron Weisner.

processes were remarkably similar. Michael and Quincy still fed off each other in that electric, symbiotic manner, but they were confident enough in each other's vision that they were able to embrace suggestions from their talented hired musical guns, guns like Eddie Van Halen, Jeff Porcaro, and Greg Phillinganes. Michael and Quincy were unequivocally in charge, but they were more like benevolent dictators, and the best idea always won out, no matter where it came from.

One of my favorite aspects of Michael and Quincy's collaboration was their flexibility and impulsiveness. They'd show up first thing in the morning, ready to finish the track they'd started the night before, but five minutes into their work, one of them would remember a bit they'd left incomplete two weeks before, and say something like, "I know how to fix the bass track." So they'd abandon their initial plan, resurrect what might have been a dead idea, and turn it into something beautiful. One, or two, or ten hours later, they'd return to their original plan as if nothing ever happened. They never wasted time, they never lost momentum, and they were fearless. They tried anything and everything, and if it didn't work, they moved on to something else without missing a beat.

As the sessions continued, it became obvious to all involved that Michael was obsessed with making history. To him, this album had to be bigger sonically, bigger culturally, and bigger in the marketplace. During the downtime in the studio, he often said, "We sold ten million last time, and if we sell ten million this time, we've failed," and when he wasn't recording, he tried to figure out how to double, or

Freddie DeMann, Larkin Arnold, and Michael Jackson at the Grammy Awards

triple, or quadruple his sales. He knew that he and Quincy were doing everything within their power to make the most appealing record they possibly could, so the question became, what next? What would take him above and beyond where he'd already been? How could he attain lofty cultural status similar to that of larger-than-life figures like the Beatles and Elvis Presley? Hell, how could he *surpass* that?

The answer was simple: MTV.

When it came to the videos for *Thriller*—especially the clip for the title cut—we all decided that we had to step it up, that the visual had to be as strong as the aural. The video had to be as memorable as the song and required a reevaluation of the entire video concept. So we decided to make movies. We wanted to do what hadn't done before.

John Landis, who directed *Animal House*, and, more pertinently for our purposes, *An American Werewolf in London*, was pretty much the only person Michael envisioned bringing the dancing zombie concept to life. But John was hot, and it would cost us. Typically, the record label pays for video production, and the money is taken from the artist's promotional budget. This isn't an issue when you make videos like "Billie Jean" and "Beat It," which weren't particularly expensive, as the content was fueled by Michael himself, rather than lots of special effects and costumed extras. But "Thriller" was more than a video. It was a mini movie, and what with the dancing zombies, Landis's fee, the special effects, and the wardrobing, it turned out to be considerably pricier than your typical video, so pricey, in fact, that Michael had to go out-of-pocket to cover the costs that Epic wouldn't. I would've told him that was a bad idea—singers don't pay for their videos—but I knew that would've been a waste of my time and my breath. When Michael wanted to do something, he did it, and you could talk to him until you were blue in the face, but you were never going to change his mind.

As preproduction continued, however, I thought, *You know what? Mike's right. This is the next logical step. The train is moving, and jumping off now would be foolish. If this is gonna work—and I can't imagine it won't—we'll go even beyond the stratosphere.*

Michael was flying higher than high. *Thriller* had gone platinum 15 times over and was still flying out of the stores to the tune of a million copies a week.* His videos ruled the airwaves, his concerts were beyond sold out, and he was the most iconic entertainer on the planet. You'd think that my job was safe, right?

Well, you'd be wrong. Despite the fact that I played a role in two albums that made him the most famous person on the planet, despite the fact that I helped put together two world tours that earned him millions upon millions of dollars, despite the fact that I'd guided him through projects like the audiobook of *E.T.*, I was on my way out. And guess who was behind it?

In 1984, with the *Thriller* train still running full speed, Freddy and I were again summoned to Hayvenhurst for yet another meeting. When I arrived, Michael, Joe, and the brothers were all seated on a sofa in the family room . . . and the brothers were all wearing sunglasses. *Shit,* I thought, *another goddamn sunglasses meeting.* Standing behind the sofa with a shit-eating grin was none other than the slimiest promoter in history, Don King. I shouldn't have been surprised. Joe and Don could've been born to the same parents. They were two peas in a scummy pod.

Joe started right in: "I called you here to tell you that we've got this biiiiiiiig money-makin' project. And my partner here is gonna give you all the details." He then pointed to King, but before King could say a word, Joe continued: "We're gonna do the biggest tour ever," he said. "Not the biggest black tour. Not the biggest white tour. The biggest tour,

---

* *Thriller* went on to sell over fifty million copies and become the greatest-selling album in history, just as Michael had hoped. I recently told Quincy, "The way the record industry is now, you sure as hell don't have to worry about anybody beating that record."

Ron Weisner and ET. I went with Michael Jackson to shoot the cover of the *E.T. Storybook* album.

period. Everybody's on board, Michael, too. But we're gonna look out for Michael, and we're gonna look out for you guys, and that's the way it's gonna be."

My first thought: *Pretty impressive on Joe's part that he didn't let a bigmouth like Don King get a word in edgewise.* My second thought: *How the hell did they convince Michael?* I knew the brothers would sign off on this in a heartbeat, but I thought that by now, Michael would know better. If I were to theorize, I'd guess that King gave each of them, Joe included, a wad of cash—maybe a hundred grand, maybe a million, who knows—then told them all they had to do to make more was to convince Michael to do the tour, because King knew that without Michael, none of it would happen. Even they weren't dumb enough to believe anyone would pay hundreds of dollars to see the Jacksons without Michael.

To me, for Michael, this was a horrible idea. It was a take-the-money-and-run kind of project that would've taken time and energy away from his own work. And I was certain that the promoters involved were Joe's scumbag buddies—King probably threw a few new scumbags into the mix—and it wouldn't reflect well on him. Considering the personalities involved, I knew it would be a logistical nightmare.*

The question was, how did they convince Michael to abandon a project that made him an international icon? Again, if I were to theorize, I'd say it involved both psychological and physical threats. I pictured the brothers telling him how awful he was for choosing his own career over his blood. I pictured Joe shoving Michael into a corner, getting in his face, and telling him, "You fucking do what I tell you to do, or else." And I pictured Michael—the most famous person in the world—not having the self-confidence or balls to tell them no.

....

* And I was right. Thousands upon thousands of seats went unsold, some of the dates were cancelled, and venues were switched and then the date was cancelled. Michael, to his credit, bailed before the circus made its scheduled trip to Europe.

I didn't speak to Michael about the tour until the following afternoon. (He called me at the house* a couple of hours after the meeting to discuss something totally unrelated. I didn't bring up the meeting, just to see if he would. He didn't.) As we sat in the studio at the back of his house, I tried my damndest to talk him out of it. "Mike," I said, "if you go on this tour, it will be the biggest mistake you'll make in your life. You've taken fifteen steps forward, and if you put yourself in the middle of that train wreck, you'll take fifteen hundred back. Look what you've accomplished. Don't jeopardize that. What you and Quincy delivered turned out to be bigger than you could've possibly dreamed." (Quincy, I should mention, also tried to convince Michael to skip the tour and continue moving forward creatively. But at that point, their relationship was strained to the point that Michael wouldn't listen to his old mentor.) "I know you want to be loyal and supportive to your brothers, but you can't allow them and Joe to run your life. You have to find a way to stand up to them. They're going to destroy everything you've worked so hard to build. This is the kiss of death, the demise of your . . . your . . . your *empire*. You've gotta make a stand for yourself. And, Michael, this isn't about me. I have no vested interest in whether you do this tour or whether you don't. I'm telling you this as a friend. And I'll do whatever I can to help you deal with Joseph and your brothers."

But as has always been the case, once Michael Jackson made up his mind about something, he wasn't budging.

....

* Whenever Michael called the house and my wife answered the phone, he'd say, "Hello, is Ron Weisner there?" Never, "Hi, it's Michael. Is Ron around?"

Had Michael given any sign of being on the fence—had I thought I could guide him to the right path—I'd have found a way to shut down the *Victory* tour. I could've done my due diligence and learned who was going to get paid under the table before, during, and after the tour. I could've shown Michael how much money was going to be taken from his pocket. I could've made a goddamn pie chart showing him just how badly he was going to get screwed. But I knew it wouldn't be worth my time, effort, or money . . . and, yes, it would've cost me more than a few cents to get this information, but I was willing to go out-of-pocket for Michael. But I knew his fear of Joe and his loyalty to his brothers trumped facts and logic.

I'll never find out exactly how Joe Jackson convinced Michael to fire me. Maybe he put together what Michael thought was a good career blueprint. Maybe he said something about how we white Jews were stealing his money. Maybe he beat the shit out of him. I have no idea, and, frankly, I don't care enough to try to find out. The psychic damage Joe caused Michael happened so long ago, and was so deeply embedded, that a team of genius shrinks would find it impossible to piece it together, and doubly impossible to fix.

I received the termination letter in the afternoon at the office. It was pretty cut and dried: I was fired, but I would still receive my percentage of any projects I'd worked on, yadda yadda yadda. Was I disappointed? You bet.

Was I pissed off? Yes.

Was I surprised? Not one bit.

I was broken up about the whole thing, more so than I would have suspected. Then again, I had given everything

I had to the guy. I fought for him, I cried with him, I celebrated with him, and I was at his beck and call. I wasn't there some of the time; I was there *all* the time. Anyone would be broken up. I had to talk with him. I wasn't going to let him get away without some sort of closure.

I talked to Michael on the phone at least twenty times a day, and he was never out of touch. He had three numbers: a private line, a *very* private line, and a very *very* private line, and he never didn't take my call.

I called the private line: "The number you have reached has been disconnected." I slammed down the phone.

I called the *very* private line: "The number you have reached has been dis . . . " Slam.

I called the very *very* private line: "The number you . . ." *Slam.*

At some point after the six times I'd last spoken to him, he'd killed all three of his phones just to avoid me. I knew it would be pointless to go to his house. If he was hiding from me via telephone, there's no way he would've spoken to me in person.

So that was the end for me and Michael Jackson.* At least for the time being.

....

* It wasn't the end for Michael, obviously, but certainly the beginning of the decline. Quincy Jones was done with Michael, so he didn't have a hand in Michael's next album, *Bad,* an album that sold well, but nowhere near as well as *Thriller.* From there, the albums sold progressively less, and I don't think anyone will argue that the reason was because they weren't nearly as good as their predecessors, and I'd argue that the reason they weren't as good is because Michael pushed away so many of the people who cared about him as a person and an artist (e.g., Quincy), replacing them with people who wanted to pick his pocket. As for his personal life, I wasn't privy to what was going on, so I can only speculate, but I choose not to. Someone else can write that book.

Fast forward one year. I was backstage at the Shrine Auditorium, suffering through one of the thousands of award shows that infest Los Angeles each year. While walking down the long hallway leading to the dressing rooms, I saw Michael's main security man, Bill. I called to him, "Hey, Bill. How you doing, man?"

He gave me a half-wave, then turned around and marched into one of the dressing rooms. I can't imagine what he was telling Michael: Maybe "Ron Weisner's here, and he's gonna come after you, so don't go anywhere without me." Or "Ron Weisner's here. Maybe you should go and say hello." Or "Ron Weisner's here. You want me to mess him up?"

But I couldn't worry about it because I had to get to one of the dressing rooms at the end of the hall. Just as I walked past Michael's dressing room, the door opened; it was Bill. Just for the hell of it, I asked him, "Is Mike in there?"

"Yeah. Go on in."

I stepped through the threshold, and there he was, my old compadre, the King of Pop. Without so much as a hello, I told him, "You know what, man? You're the most creative person I've ever known in my life, by far. But you have no balls." And then I turned around and walked out.

Two days later, at home, the phone rang: "Hello."

"Ron, I'm so sorry. It didn't have to happen this way."

"Well, it did, Mike. It did happen this way because you instigated it. So don't give me that. You did this. Bottom line, you didn't make a stand to deal with your old man, and I paid the price."

After a second, he repeated, "I'm so sorry."

"There's a lot of things I'm sorry about, too, Mike."

He hemmed and hawed for a few minutes, not saying anything particularly substantial, then hung up the phone. From that moment on, Michael wanted me back in his life. And how do I know that? Because he went back to calling me twenty times a day. Sometimes he asked for advice, sometimes he played me a bit of music, and sometimes he just wanted to say hello. I took his calls, and our conversations were always civil, but there was a lack of depth to our interaction, because I wanted it that way. I could be friendly with him, but if he wouldn't apologize—if he wouldn't step up and be a man—there was no way it could ever go back to the way it was. And that was unfortunate for him, because, believe me, he needed some guidance. He sure as hell wasn't going to get that with my replacement, Frank Dileo, a talented, well-connected guy, but not a guy who was particularly nurturing. And if anyone needed nurturing, it was Michael Jackson.

You see, when I managed Michael, his life was productive and relatively smooth, because I made sure he had both unconditional support and a bullshit detector. The biggest problems tended to be centered around his eccentricities— plastic surgeries, skin lightening, and so on—but after I left, things went downhill. Neverland Ranch, the sprawling estate where he lived between 1988 and 2005, was a money pit. It was about 3,000 acres and featured a full-blown zoo and a huge amusement park—it was a mini Disneyland, and considering how he felt about Disneyland, there was pretty much no way he'd be talked out of letting that go. And he should have, because the upkeep of the house—hell, it wasn't a house, it was a *city*—cost him about a million dollars per week. Also, his spending was out of control, and I bet that no one could tell you what it was that he was buying. It was just . . . *stuff*. He had storage facilities all over Los Angeles filled with . . . *stuff*, the detritus of his career: billboards, stages, props, everything. He was a hoarder before there were hoarders. His monthly storage costs were six figures, so you're looking at over a million dollars a year.

The vibe inside the Neverland house was *off*. Michael didn't like bright lights, so it was always dark, and there was always some sort of nasty animal smell, usually coming from the snake. If you said anything about the snake, he offered to show you how it ate a mouse, then explained, "It takes two days to digest!"

Near the end, he drifted further and further away from society. He stopped trusting anyone and alienated most of the people who still cared about him, Quincy Jones being among the notable. And he needed someone like Quincy in his life, someone who could positively channel his creativity and quirkiness, to take that energy and turn it into something beautiful. He also needed—and apologies if this comes across as egotistical—someone like me who had the balls to tell him how things really were, to tell him that he was coming across to the world as more than eccentric, to tell him that his father was a leech, to tell him to get it the fuck together.

But that safety net was gone, and he went adrift. He closed ranks and became a terminal loner, allowing himself to sink into a world that was, for lack of better words, weird, depressing, and toxic.

I stayed in touch with Michael until the end, regularly visiting him at his house, where he'd play me tunes that he'd recorded in his home studio. But at that point, Michael rarely finished anything. It was a snatch of melody, an instrumental hook here, a chorus there, a bass line or two, but never a complete song. (But there was always a whole lot to listen to, because he remained a creative dynamo. He might not have been as obsessive as he was in the 1980s, but he *worked,* even when he wasn't healthy, which was most of the time.)

Had he taken care of himself throughout his adult life, and had he not poured down so many of those goddamn pills, and had he not burnt bridges with the Quincy Joneses of the world, there's no reason he couldn't have consistently made music that equaled, if not surpassed, *Off the Wall* and *Thriller,* both in quality and sales figures. I firmly believe if he'd have simply eaten well, taken his vitamins, avoided incorrectly prescribed prescription drugs, and associated with people who cared about him as a person rather than a massive celebrity or an ATM, he'd still be here now. I mean, look at a guy like Bruce Springsteen. He was born nine years before Michael, and he's a bull, as vital as ever in concert and in the studio, because he eats well, exercises, stays focused, and works hard. It's that simple. But Michael didn't want to hear it.

About two weeks before he died, while he was gearing up for his *This Is It* comeback tour, I started hearing whispers that things were more off than usual. Word was that he looked awful, worse than he ever had, but AEG, the company promoting the tour, wasn't going to cancel the shows in order to give him time to get well. They hired a doctor, Conrad Murray, to nurse Michael back to health, which, in this case, meant pumping him full of ostensibly rejuvenative pills. In reality, it was a death cocktail, and had AEG (a) used a real doctor, and/or (b) called off the tour, the poor guy might've survived. But in AEG's mind, Murray's job was to make sure Michael was up and running so the shows—which had already garnered millions of dollars in ticket presales; fifty-plus concerts had sold out in minutes*—could go on.

A few days before Michael passed, he asked if we could get together. I was at the Shrine Auditorium, overseeing the preparation for the BET Awards, and he was at the Staples Center, rehearsing for *This Is It,* so we made plans to meet at Staples. He hadn't looked *really* healthy for a good long while, but this was at a whole other level. The first thing I thought when I saw him was, *He looks like a goddamn prisoner of war.* He was a skinny, lanky guy to start with, but he was frailer than ever; I estimated him to weigh 100 pounds. I knew he really wanted to do this tour, which was supposed to start the following week in London, and I hoped he'd be able to make it happen, because it would've helped him psychologically. But after watching him shuffle around the Staples Center stage for a few minutes, I knew there was no way he'd get to England. No way.

For that matter, I knew that was the last time I'd see him.

He had that look in his eyes, a look I've seen too many times in my life, a look of resignation, a look that said, *It's over,* and it broke my heart, because up until things headed

....

* After Michael died, AEG offered refunds, but the bulk of the ticket buyers refused, choosing instead to keep the ticket as a souvenir.

south in the early 2000s, he had it all. We all know about his singing and dancing, but everyone doesn't know about his fearlessness. There's nothing, *nothing* he wouldn't try in order to entertain a crowd of 100 or 100,000.

He was fighting demons that he never discussed with me, and even if he did, I probably wouldn't have understood. We came from vastly different worlds, but for a few years, we made a productive team. There were enormous parts of his life that I wasn't ever privy to—I never stick my nose into my clients' personal lives unless they asked me to do so—and the Michael Jackson I knew just wanted to make the best music he possibly could, music that would be enjoyed by the most people possible. The fact that many will remember his dark ending rather than his vibrant beginning and game-changing middle breaks my heart.

I was at a rehearsal for the Awards when I received the call. "I'm sorry to have to tell you this." It was LaToya.

Before she could continue, I said, "I know why you're calling. And it doesn't surprise me, but I'm really sad. I feel bad for you, I do." As soon as I hung up the phone, we completely overhauled the BET Awards, turning it into a three-hour tribute to the life and music of Michael Jackson. We focused only on the positive stuff, because what with all the controversy and accusations, the public tended to forget what Michael had given the world, and I felt it essential to remind them.

Fans and detractors alike needed to remember that in 1979, when Michael went solo, the record industry was at a crossroads. What with the lack of true superstars who could appeal to a cross section of listeners, record buyers

Ron and Gladys Knight backstage after the Michael Forever tribute concert in Cardiff, Wales, in October 2011

were becoming disengaged. And then along comes *Off the Wall,* a record that blew down doors and broke down barriers. Its impact on the marketplace was immeasurable; the numbers told us that a quality R&B-based record that embraced rock, pop, and dance would compel R&B, rock, pop, and dance fans to open their wallets. I don't think that a lot of today's artists understand that they owe Michael Jackson a debt of gratitude.

But I sure do.

And you know what else I understand? That you're worth more dead than alive.

The Michael Jackson Estate controls Michael's money, and the rest of the family, if I may put it bluntly, wants the money. Whenever anyone attempts to do something with Michael's music—as was done with the massive tribute concert I produced in Europe—they're guaranteed to be slapped with a lawsuit. (As of this writing, I'm involved in one myself, which, naturally, can't be discussed here. The only thing I'll say about it is that I need to make sure I'm in the room when all the parties and their legal representatives meet, because if they're going to piss on each other's shoes, I want them to do it in front of me. Maybe the suit will be settled in time for the sequel to this book . . . but probably not.) But, as previously mentioned, Michael is their meal ticket, and they want a piece of everything. Here's why:

When they were recording on Motown as the Jackson Five, they were minors, thus their money was controlled by Joe Jackson, money that is long gone. As for the money they've earned since, well, those guys spend, and spend, and spend, plus they've all been married multiple times, so that money is gone, too. When the topic comes up, I'm often asked, *Why do the brothers think they deserve a piece of Michael's solo output?* And my answer: *Why are you asking a rational question? Their answer would be along the lines of, We're family! Why should the Estate make these decisions?* In case you're curious, the Estate is run by three lawyers. Three busy, busy lawyers. And they're so busy in part because when Michael passed away, he was this close to declaring bankruptcy, thus the lawyers, and thus the vultures.

But here's the thing: The brothers don't have a legal leg to stand on. Everything is controlled by Michael's estate—the music, the film, the videos, his likeness, *everything*. There's a war going on, a war that was escalated a couple months after Michael passed away, with the release of *Michael*, a posthumous album from the fine folks at Epic records with what was touted as new material.

Naturally, it led to a lawsuit, and this one was particularly ugly: The family's claim is that a lot of the material on the album didn't actually come from Michael. They never made it clear who they thought made the music, but they felt comfortable enough with their theory that they brought in a musicologist to testify as to the veracity of the material.

Even when it was over, it wasn't over.

CHAPTER NINE

Madonna

Madonna would do anything to succeed. Anything she had to. And she did. It seemed at times that she was working on getting meaner.

Some of my clients were more than clients. Curtis, Gladys, and Steve were friends. Working with them wasn't a job, it was a pleasure. I couldn't wait to see them. There were others, however, I couldn't wait to get away from, people in whose presence you didn't want to spend a minute more than necessary. I'd put John Mellencamp, with whom I'd briefly worked, in the latter category. He was like a guy who'd won a twenty-million-dollar lottery and was pissed off because it wasn't twenty-one.

And then there was the Mouth from Michigan: Madonna Louise Ciccone.

It was 1982, and the dance scene was in flux; disco was all but dead, and there was a vacuum waiting to be filled. Out in New York, there were rumblings of something happening, but Weisner/DeMann Entertainment was based in Los Angeles—and I seemed to always be on an airplane—so we didn't feel the quaking. Plus we had a lot on our plates, so we can be forgiven for not knowing *exactly* what was going on in the clubs ... but we were aware that *something* was happening. We knew that the tempo on your typical dance track was faster than it had been in the disco era, and we knew that the energy at your typical dance clubs was higher than ever. I wasn't much of a club guy myself, but I recognized that we were in the midst of a transition, and I needed to pay the genre at least a little bit of attention, because you never knew. Just because no artist had busted out didn't mean there wasn't one waiting in the wings.

MTV was also in transition. Thanks in part to "Thriller," videos were marrying music with images to the point that some of these clips could be considered artistic entities unto themselves. Yes, MTV still played plenty of cheap, on-the-fly videos, but slowly, surely, many of these films were more than promotional clips. They weren't just solidifying old fans—they were attracting new ones. The world hadn't seen some of the locales where these videos were shot—Duran Duran, for example, offered viewers a look at Europe they may have never seen, a veritable teenage travelogue. The synergy happened when viewers called radio stations to request the songs they'd seen, which gave the business a sorely needed goose. It was an interesting, exciting, and unusual time, and we had to be on our toes, because dealing with transition of any kind is a challenge. But we embraced that challenge, because with new styles, new trends, and new audiences came new opportunities. In my corner of the music business, new opportunities are our lifeblood.

I was knee-deep in some Jacksons mess or another, so Freddy DeMann took the call from his old pal Seymour Stein, the head of Sire Records.* Seymour told Freddy that he'd signed a dance artist named Madonna, and she was looking for a manager, and would either of us be interested. (Why, you might ask, didn't Madonna have a manager when she was just about to sign with a label that was distributed by Warner Brothers? Because she was a New York club girl, and when you're a New York club girl, generally the only managerial choices available to you are New York club boys, guys who managed by night, worked at a gas station by day, and sold coke in the afternoon. Before Madonna, managers at our level didn't take the club world seriously.) When Seymour told Freddy what she was about—dance, style, look, MTV-ready—he asked for a tape. We gave it a listen, and it sounded . . . fine. Could she sing? No.† Was it music that would appeal to a specific audience? Yes. Was she attractive and stylish enough to be a viable entity on MTV? You bet. Did she have to potential to be a flat-out entertainer, someone who could mount a circus-like tour that would merit charging $100 per ticket? Absolutely. Was she a salable package? Definitely. Sure, her demo wasn't *What's Going On*, or *Kind of Blue*, or even *Thriller*, but, as they used to say on *American Bandstand*, it had a good beat, and you could dance to it, and considering the shifting climate, that might just be enough.

....

* Sire, it should be noted, was an independent label distributed by Warner Brothers. Citing Sire as an indie seems odd, considering they helped break enormous acts like the Ramones, Talking Heads, Depeche Mode, the Pretenders, and The Cure. And, of course, Madonna.

† I think that if pressed, Madonna would admit that at that time she wasn't a great singer. Or maybe not. Who knows with that one.

Wanting to know more, we had a couple of our people in New York confirm that she was as popular in the clubs as Seymour claimed. When we learned that yes, she was creating a buzz—and when we heard that she was a hustler who would do intense promotional and marketing work on her own behalf—we met with Seymour. He laid out Sire's plans for her, and it all sounded good, so we decided to get together with the woman herself.

At that point, I'd met hundreds of individuals in all shapes, sizes, and demeanors, so I thought I was pretty good at reading a person. At our first meeting in New York, Madonna was abrasive, the furthest thing from warm and cuddly, but there was something about her that screamed *success*, even though she hadn't done anything other than cut a pleasant enough demo. Still, it was uncomfortable being around her. I don't mind hunger and aggressiveness, but it got to a point where, well, it wasn't cool.

Two hours into the meeting, I knew Madonna would succeed. Hell, if you spent two minutes around her and you had any sense of pop culture, you knew she'd succeed. We understood immediately that she was a ground-floor artist, someone who was there first. And when you have the opportunity to work with someone who is doing something that no one else is doing—and that something is salable—you dive in. Sometimes you dive in too quickly, before you ask the right questions, but sometimes you have to have faith in your instincts and take that plunge.

Madonna herself wasn't the only reason we considered moving forward. Warner Brothers distributed Sire, and I had great relationships with their head honchos, Mo Ostin,

Lenny Waronker, and Russ Thyret. They were friends, and I trusted both their opinions and their work ethic. All three told me that the buzz around Madonna, especially in New York, was loud and legit, and Warner Brothers was going to put their promotional weight behind her, so she would be a good play. (For his part, Freddy was all-in from the get-go. He liked the glitz, glamour, and style aspect of our industry, and, to his credit, he sensed that Madonna would use glitz, glamour, style, and anything else she could think of to sell records and fill arenas.) So our lawyers met with her lawyers, and next thing you know, Madonna was in the Weisner/DeMann fold.

Right off the bat, the Madonna project felt different to me, not because her attitude was the opposite of most everyone else with whom I'd ever worked, but because she was the first artist I ever worked with who came to me without ever having played with honest-to-goodness musicians. There were others who didn't have a band; Buddah had to help Bill Withers put together a backing band, for instance, but he'd already taken to the studio with some stellar studio cats, so he knew how to sing in front of a group of musicians. Madonna, on the other hand, had done the majority of her singing to a prerecorded track. I'm not making a value judgment—a great song is a great song, no matter how it comes to fruition—but it was a clear signal that the music industry was undergoing a massive shift.

Our manager-artist relationship wasn't like that of mine and Michael's, in part because Freddy was her point person, and in part because she was who she was and looked at us as employees rather than collaborators or partners. During preproduction and production of her self-titled debut, I wasn't particularly hands-on in the studio, because I was still in Jackson hell. I interfaced some with her producer, Jellybean Benitez, a truly nice guy who somehow managed to date her for two years without hurting himself or anyone else, but, for the most part, Freddy handled the care and feeding of that first record.

I came back into the fold in 1984, during the planning stages of how to market her second album, *Like a Virgin*. I spent a lot of time with Jeff Ayeroff, the head of Warner Brothers' creative services department, a department that oversaw all of their advertising, marketing, and, most important for me, videos. (Not only did Jeff collaborate with Madonna, but also he was the company's point person for Eric Clapton and the Doobie Brothers. I won't presume to say with whom he most enjoyed working.) When it came time to discuss the video for the lead single, "Like a Virgin"—as was the case with Michael—I suggested taking a different route, using a producer and director who came from outside of the video world. This isn't to demean the video world, mind you; it's just that in my experience in this venue, different is better. Or, at the very least, different.

I don't know how it hit me, but I told Jeff, "I think we should shoot the video in Venice."

"Great! That's right down the street. It'll save us a ton of money."

"No, I don't mean Venice in LA. I mean Venice in Italy."

Jeff paused. "You know, Ron, that'll dramatically change the budget." He sounded worried. Even after her first album went multiplatinum, they were still hesitant to spend any money. Warner wasn't looking to make *Gone With the Wind.* As long as MTV played the damn thing, they didn't care what was on the screen. Eventually, they decided that unique was good, that it would be a smart investment, so they gave us the money. For a brief time, like three minutes, Madonna was happy. For her, it was a love-fest. So it was off to Venice.

Now, shooting something in Venice isn't like shooting something in, say, Pittsburgh, because (a) it's Italy, and (b) there was no place to drive, so everything had to be carried. We had to find just the right spots, which meant moving all over Venice, which meant hauling our equipment from one locale to the next on boats. I doubt you've hauled movie gear on a boat, but I'm here to tell you that it's a slow process involving multiple setups, multiple breakdowns, and multiple gondolas.

This can become a problem when your star is missing the patience gene.

Every time we packed up the cameras, she bitched. Every time we got into a boat, she bitched. Every time she had to wait for setup, she bitched. "You're all a bunch of fucking idiots," she'd tell the Italian crew, who was busting its collective hump to get her video in the can. "You're wasting my time. You're wasting our time. Now quit sticking it to me and hurry up."

I asked Freddy, "What the hell's her problem? We're in Italy. It's more fun than being in Long Island City. What does she have going on that's better than this?" He just shrugged.

The next day, whenever I looked at Madonna, she was staring right back at me, a nasty look plastered on her face.

That was nothing new, so I didn't think much of it. Right before lunch, Freddy pulled me aside and said, "I think you should leave."

"Excuse me?"

"Madonna's getting really upset. She's not happy. She doesn't want you around."

The only reason I could think of why she'd want me off the set was that she'd overheard me bitching about her bitching. "You know what," I told Freddy, "that's fine. I'm gone." I split, and I had a lovely, headache-free day in Venice.

That didn't keep me from going to her next video shoot for the second single, "Material Girl." This one was shot in LA, so if I was tossed from the set, I'd have to go back to the office rather than explore the streets of Italy, so I tried to be on my best behavior. For that matter, I decided that not only would I be on good behavior but also I'd actively help.

In 1984, unlike today, few hard news television outlets covered entertainment stories—movie premieres, awards shows, celebrity scandals—choosing instead to focus on, you know, hard news. But I had a lot of friends in LA who were television journalists, so I called a pal at the local ABC affiliate and said, "Listen, we're shooting this Madonna video. You should come down. I'll get you full access. Nobody else will have anything like this, ever." I suggested how we could position and schedule the piece, and he agreed.

When I arrived on the set, I checked out the schedule, then tracked down Madonna and told her, "I have some news people coming in to do a feature on the shoot. We have an hour break at 4:00, and they'll be here then, so meet us at your trailer. You can relax for a little bit, but it would be great for you if you could do this on-camera interview. I spoke with my friend at ABC, and what they'll do is, the day the video comes out, they'll run the interview, as well as a clip from the video. That never happens on network television."

Miracle of miracles, she agreed. When we got to break, I ran over to the trailer, knocked on her door, and called, "It's Ron! Can you come out in ten minutes?"

She opened the door, poked her head out, looked around to make certain no one could hear her, and said, "Do I have to? What did you get me into now? Is this really necessary?"

"Yeah," I said, "it *is* necessary. This is a big deal for you, and the ABC people are doing a personal favor to me, and besides, you already agreed to do it."

"I don't give a shit about *your* favors."

My face probably turned three shades of crimson. "Wait a minute," I said, "this is about you. This is about your record. This is about your career. This isn't about me. They're here to talk to you, and you can talk about anything you damn well want."

After five more minutes of verbal jousting, she did the interview. As was always the case with Madonna, when the cameras turned on her, she was terrific.

At that point, I thought, *Whenever I do anything with this girl, it's a hassle. Everything's a battle, and, yeah, she's making us money, but I have other acts whose company I enjoy. Screw this.* So I told Freddy that he was our official Madonna representative and not to bring me into something unless he was desperate.

A few months later, while my partner was dealing with his favorite client's bullshit, I was dealing with a madman lunatic named Michael Ovitz. I'd known Mike from around— I'd been in LA for long enough that I knew *everybody* from around—and word got back to me that he was starting a talent agency, Creative Artists Agency, aka CAA. Some found him difficult to deal with, but I liked the guy, and I knew he'd be a bear for his clients, so I thought it would be a good idea to get in on the ground floor. (Like Madonna, Ovitz was a ground-floor individual.) Because I'm a glutton for punishment, I got back into Madonna's world and hooked her up with Ovitz, making her CAA's first music client.

Was this a big deal? Hell, yes. Was she happy she had a legitimate talent agency to help her grow and diversify her career? Absolutely. Was she grateful that yours truly had made it happen? Grateful wasn't in her vocabulary.

I told CAA that we wanted to do a four-month tour, with fifty dates. They came back to us with venues, promoters, and fees, after which we ran some numbers and figured out how much we could shell out to mount the tour, while still getting Madonna a paycheck with which she was happy. I sent the figures to her accountant and business manager, saying, "You guys deal with this, and get back to me." Because there was no way I was going to broach the topic with her directly. She approved, and off we went.

The first show was at the Paramount Theater in Seattle, a nice four-thousand-seat venue, the perfect place to work out any kinks. An hour before the show, I went outside to get a breath of fresh air. As I stood near the theater's front entrance, I watched car after car pull up and drop off several young girls, all dressed in their Madonna-like sleeveless tops, studded black gloves, and dangling necklaces. The majority of the other attendees were a mother or a father with their kid in tow. I'd guesstimate that 75 percent of the audience was under the age of fifteen—some accompanied by their parents, some not—and the other 25 percent was gay men.

When the show started, the kids went nuts, screaming and screeching as kids are prone to do. I don't know if this was in reaction to the kids' reaction, but Madonna got raunchier than I'd ever seen her, fondling her breasts and playing with her crotch for no apparent artistic reason. Later on, she grabbed a boom box prop, straddled it, and pretended to fuck it, all while saying the filthiest stuff you can imagine. As she extolled the joys of masturbation, I scanned the crowd, taking in the adults' shocked, appalled expressions, and thought, *What the fuck.*

After the show, I tracked down Freddy and asked him, "What're we doing here? Is this how we want to be represented? Do we want to be associated with some girl who thinks it's okay to finger herself in front of a roomful of junior high schoolers?"

Freddy scoffed, "They loved it! Madonna's going to be huge!"

"Of course she is. But like I said, is this how we want to be represented? Do you want people saying, 'Boy oh boy, Ron and Freddy sure are doing a great job with that foul-mouthed, non-singing singer'?"

"You know what, Ron?" Freddy said. "This girl is the perfect storm. We've got radio, we've got the clubs, we've got video, and we've got a show. And she has no boundaries.

She'll do anything. *Anything.*"* This kind of crap went on for the entire tour. If I had a nickel for every phone call I received from a press person telling me that Madonna dropped her top during a photo session, well, I'd have a lot of nickels.

Over the next few months, Freddy and I began drifting apart, like a married couple falling into the crapper. We started off on the same page but went in different directions. It wasn't a pissing contest, full of finger-pointing and name-calling. We just weren't in the same place.

When we discussed the endgame, one of the primary issues became which of us would get which client. He knew from the start that he wasn't ever going to get a piece of the artists I was managing before he came aboard. We went down the roster, and when we got to Madonna's name, I said, "You can have her. You belong together." The second those words left my mouth, I felt like a huge, vulgar, surly, masturbating-on-stage weight had been lifted from my shoulders. As for Freddy, I think that's all he wanted to hear, because after that, our divorce was (more or less) smooth sailing.†

A goodly number of people who knew Madonna agreed with my decision, while others, whose opinions I actually respected, thought I was nuts. The naysayers' thinking was along the lines of, *How the hell could you walk away from what will amount to millions of dollars?* Well,

---

* And she'll still do anything. A few weeks before I started writing this book, she flashed her breast at a concert in Paris. I'm not a prude, but this is a woman in her fifties with a teenage daughter. Classy.

† After the final papers were signed, Freddy, for reasons I still can't fathom, decided to rent an office in my building. Those twice-a-week elevator rides were awkward, to say the least.

The View from Gladys Knight

The first time I met Madonna, she was becoming a little something something in the business, and she was cool. I don't mean cool like cold, but cool like lofty. I'm a hugger, and a HEY GIRL kind of person, but she was . . . cool. She wasn't even on the charts yet, but she must've known it was going to happen. And that's okay. Sometimes you have to have confidence in yourself. But you have to be careful how you walk that line in the music industry, because if you're not careful, you'll become something else. Me, I'd rather be good in heart and spirit than get caught up in what you shouldn't get caught up in. I'm confident in the gifts that God gave me, but my mom made sure that my head didn't get too big. Ron Weisner was also good at helping me keep my feet on the ground, even when I had a number one record. Actually, especially when I had a number one record. That's why I thought Madonna made a good choice when she went with Ron and Freddy.

When Ron gave her up to his partner, well, that impressed me, because he knew she could be something big, something huge. He gave up millions of dollars, but that's who Ron is. He's more concerned about people than money. But he's doing fine. He's still living, he's got a house, and he's driving something, and that's cool. If you achieve what you want in life, and you have enough to be comfortable, you're doing very, very well.

it's never been all about the money for me. Sure, I want to help my family have a good life, but I also want *me* to have a good life, and if Madonna were part of it, well, no amount of money was worth the headache. Besides, had I kept Madonna around, I would've had to spend considerably less time with Gladys and my other clients, who I actually enjoyed. I didn't like Madonna, and Madonna didn't like me, and there were thousands of other people and things that I would've rather dealt with, so I let Freddy have her, and everyone was happy, and I have absolutely zero regrets.

Don't get me wrong: I have a lot of respect for her as an entertainer and a businesswoman. Even though, like Joe Jackson, she was never personality-plus, I give her full credit for shrewdness, street smarts, and smart-smarts. She learned early on how to manipulate the press, how to create controversy, how to push everything up to the edge and beyond, and turn it into commercial domination. And even though she was just a kid when I first met her—twenty-three years old, tops—I knew that if she didn't implode, the sky was the limit.

And I was right. I just didn't want to be around it.

CHAPTER TEN

Winwood

If a toothbrush was properly strung, Steve Winwood could play it.

It was 1985, and there was a void out there. Sure, there was plenty of great stuff on the radio—Whitney Houston had a couple of nice songs, and Chicago was still making some pretty good music—but something was missing. Too many of the top 40 songs were over-produced. Musicians weren't given the opportunity to be musicians, and I missed that. I missed the heart. I missed the soul.

Enter Steve Winwood.

I'd always been a Winwood fan. He was one of the greatest—if not the greatest—hired guns of the late '60s and early '70s—we're talking Traffic, and the Spencer Davis Group, and Blind Faith, and Ginger Baker's Air Force. And the reason he was so sought after was his ability to fit into any musical situation, as a guitarist, a keyboardist, a vocalist . . . hell, you give the guy some dental floss, a twig, and some chewing gum, and he could make music out of it. Who wouldn't want that guy on their side?

I know I did.

I asked around, and it became clear pretty quickly that this wouldn't be the kind of thing where I called him up, introduced myself, laid out a game plan, then got him into the studio and onto the road. Steve, while one of the nicest musical geniuses you'll ever meet, wasn't easy. He's a brilliant musician—a musician's musician—and a brilliant songwriter, but back in the 1980s, he was a veritable recluse. Not one of those Howard Hughes recluses, who doesn't cut his fingernails and wears Kleenex boxes as shoes, mind you, just the kind of guy who wants to be left alone to write and record songs out of the mainstream, songs just for himself. Plus he wasn't a nineteen-year-old kid anymore, who could sling his guitar over his shoulder, throw a couple of outfits into a beat-up suitcase, and hit the road for a year or two. He'd done that for years, and he was probably exhausted. If any musician deserved to wear Kleenex boxes, it was Steve Winwood.

I understood that. I respected that. While that might have been baffling to some—*He's Steve Winwood, for cryin' out loud,* folks would think, *and if he makes a commercial record, he could mint money*—it made perfect sense to me. Like me, he valued artistic integrity over an easy payday.

But I thought I could make both happen. I thought he could deliver an album that he'd be proud of and could sell a few million copies. A grandiose idea, of course, but the question I asked myself about a hundred times a day was, *If I'm able to convince this reclusive genius to get out of his home studio and into the world, how exactly can I do this? Point A is getting him to a place where he'll cut the record that'll sound good to him and the world at large, and Point Z is a massively successful world tour, culminating with a flock of Grammy Awards. Now all I need are points B through Y.* Okay, maybe I didn't ask myself that exact question a hundred times a day, but Steve was always on my mind.

He hadn't released anything since *Talking Back to the Night* in 1982, and while the album made some noise, it didn't garner the huge sales it deserved. That's why when I took the pulse of the industry, when I asked my colleagues with the good ears whether it made sense to pursue Steve, the general reaction was, "I don't know, Ronnie. The guy hasn't had a record out in three years. He's off the map. The public wants Wham, and A-ha, and Madonna."

My first reaction: *I don't want to hear about that goddamn Madonna.*

My second reaction: *The public doesn't always know what it wants until they get it.*

It wasn't easy tracking him down. He lived way outside of London, in a town called Gloucestershire, in a beautiful home that was built in the 1600s. There was a barn just off the house, which housed his studio; any music he made was cut there, and he played all the instruments. From what I understood, he was tinkering with some songs, and the fact that he was tinkering even just a little meant there was a chance he'd tinker a lot. If he wasn't tinkering at all, I don't know if I would've bothered.

Even though I had a bit of cachet in the industry, I probably couldn't get through to Steve without some help, and even if I managed to get through to him, there's no guarantee he'd take my call. Fortunately, I knew a few people in England—specifically Chris Blackwell from Island Records (Steve's label since 1977) and producer Trevor Horn, who I knew via another one of my acts, Frankie Goes to Hollywood—who facilitated an introduction. Honestly, I'm not sure why Steve agreed to meet with me. He didn't have a manager, and that was by choice; he wasn't working, so in his mind, a manager wasn't really necessary.

Always cordial, Steve welcomed me into his home, and we chatted for a good part of an entire day. When we got around to discussing the resumption of his career, he groaned, "Ahhh, I have two more records left on my Island contract, and I don't want to . . . with Blackwell . . . and . . . and . . ."

I knew what he was getting at. Chris Blackwell went to the Joe Jackson School of Accounting, whose motto is, "One for you and six for me." Steve was too nice of a guy to rake Blackwell over the coals, so I shifted gears: "Look, you're an amazing artist with an amazing voice, and there's a void out there, and I think you can fill it."

He was silent. Not in a rude way, just thoughtful. Our day came to an end an hour later, with nothing resolved.

I flew back to England a couple weeks later to give it another shot. (I don't know how many times I flew from Los Angeles to England and back again in pursuit of Steve Winwood, but it made my Buddah-era NYC-to-LA commutes seem like quick jaunts around the block.)

Eventually, I felt at ease enough with him that I was comfortable offering a suggestion: "If you move forward, I don't know if this one-man-band thing of yours is the best

The View from Steve Winwood

I don't know how many times he flew out to see me, but it seemed like a lot. I hope he had other business while he was there. If it was just to see me, I owe him an apology.

way to proceed. I think if you put together a collection of the best of the best musicians, you could make more than a record. You could make a statement."

As he chewed that over, I thought, *Man, do I have a pair of balls, or what? Here's schmucky me telling Steve Winwood what to do.* Fortunately, when it came to music, Steve was willing to put anything and everything on the table, so for the rest of the day (and evening), we discussed collaboration and compromise, two topics with which, thanks to Quincy Jones, I was quite familiar. "If we find you the right producer, you can get the exact sounds you want, and you don't have to do it all yourself, and you might even find somebody who can add something to the mix that you hadn't even considered. It takes the pressure off you, and increases the opportunity to create something richer than you could ever imagine." I steeled myself, then said, "And I think you have to leave your home studio to make that happen. You've closed yourself off from the world. You're in this constrictive environment, and if you get out there, nothing but good things will happen."

Much to my pleasure and surprise, he not only agreed but also asked me if I had any specific producers in mind.

And I did: Russ Titleman, a young veteran who'd worked with everyone from George Harrison, to Paul Simon, to Randy Newman, to Chaka Khan, to George Benson. As Steve was a true musician's musician, he was impressed with Russ's credentials. When I looked into his eyes, I could see the wheels spinning.

After I flew home, Russ sent Steve samples of his material, and the two of them opened up a dialogue. They clicked both personally and professionally, so I hauled Russ to England for my next recruitment trip. As the day progressed, Steve seemed to become more amenable to not just getting back to work but getting back to work *with* someone. Come nighttime, I was confident enough to ask Steve, "Do you want to discuss a schedule?"

He did. "When do you want me in New York?" he asked.

I felt as if I'd just won a Grammy Award.

From soup to nuts, it took over two years to bring the album *Back in the High Life* to fruition. To give you some perspective, today a group can write, record, mix, and release a terrific-sounding album in about a month. And even someone like Beyoncé, whose albums are produced to the nth degree, can get a piece of quality product ready to go in nine-plus months if necessary. This isn't to say that things were necessarily better back then. Just different. At any rate, I preferred taking it slow, as did Steve. (Given the chance, I'm sure every musician in the world would love the gift of time. Around 1990, things became very *rush rush rush*.) That allowed us—and when I say us, I mean mostly Steve and Russ—the time to figure out the texture, to shape the songs, to hire the perfect backing musicians, stellar jazz cats like Randy Brecker, Bob Mintzer, and George Young, and heavyweight keyboardists like Arif Mardin and Rob Mounsey, and, lest we forget, guitarist greats like Joe Walsh and Nile Rogers. Also, as noted, Russ had produced a few things for Chaka Khan, which was part of the reason we were able to land her for a guest spot on "Higher Love." The artistic success of that tune was unexpected, to say the least. Who'd have thought the woman who sang "Tell Me Something Good" and the guy who sang "Gimme Some Lovin'" would mesh so wonderfully? But it worked. I have no idea why, but if I did, I probably wouldn't give away my secrets. Music managers have to keep some things to themselves.

It was a great puzzle, and by taking our time to put it together, we came up with a finished product that was both of its era and timeless, a record that far exceeded my lofty expectations, one of the most gratifying projects with which I've been associated.

The magic continued when we took the show to the road. (Once the record was completed, Steve had no issues with touring. He was back in the game and ready to show the world.) He didn't love the touring aspect of touring—who does?—but onstage, making music, he came to life in a way I never could've imagined during those first hesitant meetings in Gloucestershire. He rediscovered how much he loved playing with other terrific musicians, but he also rediscovered his love of performing, of putting on a *show*.

It's one thing to hear Steve overdub a dozen instruments on an album, but it's a whole other thing to see it live, to bask in his musicianship. During a typical instrumental breakdown, he'd lean down and pick up a ukulele.

Then a banjo. Then a bass. Then a guitar. Then he'd hit the keyboard. If there was a didgeridoo within arm's reach, I'm sure he'd snatch it up and play the shit out of it. Whenever I saw him do that—and I saw that a *lot*—I thought, *This guy is the consummate musician.* I wasn't the only one who felt that way, as borne out by the album's five Grammy awards.

In retrospect, I played only a small, small part in Steve's comeback. All I did was give him a nudge, and he did the rest. I was merely along for the ride, and what a ride it was.

The View from Steve Winwood

I can say unequivocally that my, I guess you'd call it, resurgence, in the 1980s had a lot to do with Ron Weisner.

Manager-artist relationships are usually born out of necessity. They come about because the manager needs an artist, or the artist needs a manager, or they need each other. Once in a rare while, it develops into something more than a business union of mutual convenience. I've had some not-so-pleasant experiences with managers, and that made me think very carefully about what I did and didn't want out of a representative. A good manager wears many hats: He has a business hat, a nursemaid's hat, a parental hat, and a psychiatric hat. And I mention the last one because many artists are quite emotionally unstable due to the very fact of who they are and what they do; I don't think I'd include myself among them, and I don't think I had to test Ron in that respect.

My career has had a few different phases, and I'd been successful, but I didn't have that big success when I was young, which can be slightly destabilizing for an artist. But the fact that I'd been an artist for over twenty years possibly made me a bit easier for Ron to deal with. Still, Ron had to get to know my quirks, and, in doing that, he proved to have an incredible insight and feel for what an artist needed and wanted. He had a genuine idea of what was best for me.

I was always more of a musician than a personality. Some artists are personalities who happen to be good at some sort of music, but I started life as a musician, playing different instruments in different styles. I also had trouble becoming a front man. I could be a bandleader, but being a bandleader is considerably different than being a front man; Ron delicately steered me into the direction in which I could do both, and enjoy both. It was astute of him to understand that, and for that, I'm eternally grateful.

CHAPTER ELEVEN

McCartney

If there's any musician who should be allowed to be as arrogant and egotistical as he'd like, it's Paul McCartney. But he's not.

When I was a kid, I ate, drank, and slept soul and R&B, but—like most everyone else with a working pair of ears—the Beatles were one of the groups that shaped my musical life. I watched their appearances on *The Ed Sullivan Show,* I wished like hell I could've gone to their Shea Stadium show, and I listened to the records over, and over, and over again. They were from a world entirely different than mine, but their lyrics, their melodies, and their instrumental prowess spoke to me as if they were my next-door neighbors. Listening to the Beatles was a great learning experience. Their whimsy with words meant more than most of my English lessons, and their instrumentation meant more than music class. (I mean, you didn't run into too many flugelhorns or French horns on the streets of Queens.) It's this sense of depth that compelled me to turn my radio dial from station to station, hoping to hear a new Beatles tune. After they broke up, I followed their solo careers; if you were a music person, you had to. Individually, all four of them had some terrific material, but it never approached the sounds they concocted when they were together.

I first met Paul McCartney when he recorded with Michael Jackson back in 1983, and, frankly, I was nervous. You don't know what to expect when you meet *anybody*, but when it's a Beatle, well, you're dealing with some seriously unchartered territory. Compounding the discomfort, I was a fan, and when you're in my position, it's difficult meeting someone whom you've rabidly admired for the majority of your life. I *wanted* to tell him how much his music meant to me, but I *had* to be professional and do my job. It's like my head was split in two.

Paul made that problem disappear when he gave me a hug and said, "Ronnie, glad to meetcha, mate!" Eventually, I found out that he wasn't going out of his way to make me comfortable. That's just the way he is, zero ego, zero attitude. He was genuinely glad to meet me.

The next time I saw Paul was right after *Thriller* first went platinum. I was in the UK, and it dawned on me that it would be nice to give Paul a platinum record while I was in town, in part because I'm certain his appearance on the record sold us an extra 100,000 copies. We met at the offices of his publishing company, and when I gave him the plaque, he was appreciative, even though, as witnessed by what was happening on the walls of his office, he had plenty of his own.

Before I left the office, Paul's manager, Richard Ogden, pulled me into his office. After some pleasant chitchat, Richard told me, "Paul's planning his record for next year, *Flowers in the Dirt,* and he wants to be aggressive about it." Professionally speaking, Paul is an interesting case. Every two or three years, he'll put out a record, and sometimes he'll do a tour, and sometimes he won't. Then there are other times he'll tour even when he doesn't have a new record to support. Basically, he tours when he wants to, when he's feeling inspired and creative, and that's impressive to me, because he doesn't have to tour at all. "He wants to be really aggressive this time," Richard said. "There have been ups and downs, and we want this to be an up. Paul and I are interested in having you oversee the entire project in North America."

If a Beatle asks you to join him, you join him, and you don't ask questions.

The work itself was similar to all my other acts—liaise with the record label, hammer out tour logistics, plot a promotion strategy, smooth out any road bumps along they way, the usual drill—the key difference being Paul was a Beatle. Sure, Michael was an icon, but Paul's star was in another galaxy.

Eventually, though, I was comfortable enough with Paul that I treated him the same as I would any other client, and that meant being honest and never holding back. As was the case with Michael, and Gladys, and everyone, I offered up my thoughts about his album-in-progress. (Me, giving a Beatle musical advice? Absurd.) Sometimes he agreed, sometimes he disagreed, and sometimes he argued, but he always, *always* listened.

I also didn't know what to expect from Paul's wife, Linda. For years, the word on the street was that she was a witch, and a control freak, and a nightmare. The first time

Linda McCartney backstage, Paul McCartney tour

we met, I decided that her reputation was ridiculous—she was lovely, gracious, and kind, just like her husband. *But*, I thought, *maybe the word on the street is true. Maybe I just caught her on a good day.* It turned out that with Linda, there were no bad days. She was, without fail, sunshine on a cloudy day, always eager to discuss art, her kids, or the weather. Linda McCartney was one of the most misunderstood people in the world.

When we hit the road to support *Flowers in the Dirt*, I reached out to my numerous radio connections across the country to line up interviews. (Those were easy phone calls: "Do you want to have an interview with Paul McC ..." They'd say yes before I could say "artney.") Going to and from those interviews was always a treat, because (a) Paul and I had the opportunity to talk music,* and (b) he was, without fail, a joy to work with—professional, energized, and punctual. *Especially* punctual. If Paul said he was going to do something—a meeting, a signing, an interview, whatever—you knew it was going to happen, and you didn't have to give it a second thought. "I don't like hanging people up," he'd say as we hustled to make it on time to yet another radio appearance.

Traveling with Michael Jackson was an adventure, but traveling with a Beatle was surreal. Paul and Linda had a house in Tucson, and when they came to the states to discuss the tour, Quincy, Michael, and I went to Arizona for a visit. They picked us up at the airport and took us to their favorite local Mexican restaurant. The place was tiny, and what few people were there conspicuously gawked at Paul, but none approached him. Fans felt that Michael, as eccentric as he was, was approachable, but they were afraid to initiate a conversation with Paul, who's just about the most easygoing famous person you'll ever meet.

And then there was the time that Paul was doing a week of shows at Soldier Field in Chicago, and they only had one day off, so they decided to have their kids fly into town.

....

* Paul was a walking musical encyclopedia, but I once blew him away when I recalled that Phil Phillips sang "Sea of Love." That's something he remembers to this day.

Paul McCartney and Ron Weisner

Linda called me early that morning and said, "I'm sorry to bother you, Ron, but the kids would like to go to the movies with us." (That's the kind of woman Linda McCartney was, always worried that she was bothering you.) "I'm not comfortable with Paul going somewhere with a big crowd, so I bought out the movie theater across the street from the hotel. We haven't seen the kids in a while, and I want them to enjoy themselves." Some might look at that as being overly extravagant, but I look at it as a nice lady using her available resources to be the best mother she possibly could.

On a personal and spiritual level, whizzing around the country with Paul was a dream. The concerts were crowded, the band sounded great, and a good time was had by most, if not all. But in the music industry, nothing is ever as great as it seems, because our business is fickle. When you're hot, you're hot, and everyone loves you—your old fans, your new fans, your record label, the press, promoters, retailers, everyone—but when you haven't had a hit in a year, or two, or three, no one wants to know you. This is the case even when you're at the level of Paul McCartney.

From 1983 on, Paul's record sales in the United States had been inconsistent, at best. None of his albums reached the top ten, and his only solo number one single was "Coming Up," and that was way back in 1980. ("Ebony and Ivory" and "Say Say Say" both topped the chart, but those were duets with, respectively, Stevie Wonder and Michael Jackson.) So garnering momentum and record sales for *Flowers in the Dirt* was an uphill battle. Both Paul and Richard Ogden, to their credit, knew going into the project that that was going to be the case, which is why they hired me. But there was only so much I could do.

The perception surrounding Paul was always, *His new stuff isn't as good as his old stuff,* and on a certain level, I doubt he'd deny that. Think about "Yesterday." Think about "Let it Be." Think about "Michelle." He knew he couldn't compete with that, which was why 75 percent of that tour's set list was Beatles material. But he believed in his new music, and he wanted to keep making more new music, so he kept plugging along. How could you not admire that? The guy who wrote or cowrote some of the most enduring tunes in pop music history doesn't want to rest on his laurels, even if by not doing so, he opens himself up to shots from fans and critics alike.

Paul's label wasn't much help. All they cared about was how much flesh he'd press, how many interviews he'd schedule, and how many public appearances he'd make. And while Paul had a healthy appreciation for the business side of the record business—Lee Eastman, Linda's father, played a big role in helping Paul understand the importance of playing the game—he was, first and foremost, a musician, and, to me, it was sacrilegious that the execs would make Paul come to their offices and discuss nothing but logistics. If you have Paul McCartney in a room, you have to ask him about music, because (a) he's a genius, (b) that's what he loves to talk about, and (c) *he's Paul McCartney!* When you're in the presence of a Beatle, the conversation has to have more substance than, "On Thursday at 5:25 a.m., we need you to be available to speak with Wacky Wally Warthog from radio station WHOG in Rantoul, Illinois, then we've scheduled forty-two interviews, beginning at noon, and ending at midnight." Nothing creative was ever discussed.

I'd sit in these meetings—and there were a lot of them—and think, *This is the beginning of the end of the record business I know.* It wasn't about making the best record, but rather playing the numbers game. On the way out, I'd inevitably tell Paul, "Sorry about that, man. It's a different time." He'd nod, then quietly say, "I know."

Paul didn't need to put up with that. He didn't need the headache, and he certainly didn't need the money. But he endured the bullshit for one reason: He loved making music. He didn't have to record, and he didn't need to tour, but entertaining was part of his DNA. It's what he lives for. It keeps his mind and soul going. This is why his concerts are so phenomenal. This is why he'll never retire.

I've learned something from each of my clients, and even though I was with Paul for only a brief time, his lessons were among the most impactful. From Paul McCartney, I learned that you must persevere not only when things are at their worst but also when they're at their best. From Paul McCartney, I learned that it's possible to balance your show business with your personal life, and remain at the top of your game in both. From Paul McCartney, I learned that entertainment is a noble profession in which you can effect change and spread peace and love.

And from Paul McCartney, I learned that even after the 1,531st hearing, "Drive My Car" is still a great song.

CHAPTER TWELVE

Production

It was easy to walk away, but impossible to stay far away.

John Mellencamp is a talented guy—I'll never take that away from him—but one tough client. Okay, maybe "tough" is an understatement. He was a pain in the ass.

As was the case with all of my clients, I gave 200 percent for him, for which he was rarely, if ever, grateful. For that matter, he was always pissed about something, and I'd inevitably hear about it during one of his many early morning phone calls. John wasn't much for pleasantries; he wasn't the kind of person who would say, "Hi, Ron, it's John." No, during his calls, he went straight into complaining mode: "Why aren't I seeing any advertising in Omaha? Why aren't my sales in Texas better? The monitor guy at the Miami show was incompetent . . . " It's an understatement to say that John Mellencamp was not personality-plus.

Early one morning sometime in late 2000, the phone rang. I looked at the clock: 4:26 a.m. I thought, *Fucking Mellencamp*, then picked up the phone. (He was the only person who ever called that early, but he lived in Indiana and didn't take time zones into consideration.) After thirty minutes of some vintage Mellencamp whining, I hung up the phone, jumped into my car, and went for a ride.

As I drove north out of Los Angeles on the PCH at 90 mph, I started talking to myself, complaints along the lines of, "I'm done with this shit. I don't want to do this anymore. It's not worth it. It's not fun." The question became, was I willing to move on? Was I willing to sacrifice everything I'd built to get away from the headaches? See, the headaches were minor, but there were so goddamn many of them, and it added up to one hell of a migraine. But there was precedent: I'd moved from MGM/Verve to Buddah, and that worked out. And I'd moved from Buddah to Weisner Entertainment, and that worked out. The thing is, with both of those moves, I was moving to *something*, so if I was going to move now, I'd need a plan.

I hit San Luis Obispo, some three and a half hours away from LA, where I popped a U-turn and headed home. The conversation with myself continued, with a change in topic: "What am I gonna do now? What have I done? What do I know how to do? I've helped mount live shows. I've helped put together videos and video shoots. I've worked on all these television shows. I'm gonna call somebody."

When I returned home, I immediately picked up the phone and called my old friend from the Sha Na Na television show, Pierre Cossette. Aside from producing the Grammy Awards telecast,* Pierre had his hand in everything

----

* When the Grammys first hit the television airwaves in 1971, Pierre paid for it out of his own pocket for the first two years. Talk about foresight. And balls.

from TV, to movies, to Broadway. If anybody had a good idea as to how I could best monetize my past experience, he'd be the guy, so I invited myself to his office for a meeting the following morning.

The next day at his office, as is my wont, I cut right to the chase: "Pierre, I've known you for a long time, and I have a question: Do you have a project coming up that you need a producer for? Because I'm interested. I've never done it before, so if you don't want to pay me, you don't have to. If you like what I do, I have a couple of ideas for other projects."

He didn't even blink. "Actually, could you come back tomorrow at 2:00? I have a meeting you might want to be at."

The following afternoon, I strolled into Pierre's conference room, where he introduced me to Bob Johnson. The name sounded familiar, but I couldn't quite piece it together.

Bob stuck out his hand and said, "Ron Weisner. I know you. You used to manage Michael Jackson."

I didn't want Bob to know that I didn't know who he was, so I shook his hand and said, "Great to meet you. I know you've done some wonderful things yourself."

He smiled, said, "Thanks. Very kind of you to say." (*Phew,* I thought. *Got away with that one.*) Then he turned to Pierre and said, "I came here today to meet with the guy who produces the Grammys, to find out if you could build an award show for my network."

And then it dawned on me: Bob Johnson created Black Entertainment Television, aka BET.

Pierre asked me, "What do you think about that, Ron?"

"Sounds like a great idea."

"Would you be interested in doing it?"

"Sure! Why not?" I'd never before produced a television show on that level, but before I started at MGM, I'd never worked at a record label, and before I started at Buddah, I'd never run a record label, and before I opened Weisner Entertainment, I'd never managed, so I wasn't afraid of playing on a field on which I'd never set a foot. Nervous, sure, but scared, no. Pierre and Bob worked out a deal, and next thing you know, I'm a producer.

Soon thereafter, Pierre took ill, so his son John took over the company. Where Pierre was experienced and professional, John, who used to be a runner on the Sha Na Na show, wasn't. Pierre was a one of a kind, and it would've been difficult for *anybody* to step into his shoes, but Pierre was comfortable with his son running the ship, and it was his company, so who was I to complain? It wasn't like I had any experience, either, so I went to work on the BET Awards and hoped for the best.

The first BET Awards ceremony was held at the Bally Hotel in Las Vegas, home of the Jubilee Show, the venerable revue featuring dozens of feather-wearing, high-kicking showgirls. The stage in the tacky room is as big as a king-size bed, which didn't send a great message. Because we were the new kids on the block, the only way we could get any acts to perform was to call in some favors. (At BET, it seemed like it was always Favor Time.) We managed to pull it off, as we did the following year at the Paris Hotel in Vegas, a place with an adult-size stage that allowed us to present an adult-size show. That was good enough for Bob. It became official: The BET Awards was going to be an

Backstage at BET awards. Loni and Muhammad Ali.

annual event, and the following year, we were taking it to Los Angeles.

The next four years, we held it at the Kodak Theater, then it was moved to the Shrine Auditorium for the following eight, and each year, it got bigger and bigger, and the hosts grew in stature; we started out with the likes of Mo'Nique—a perfectly talented woman, mind you—before graduating to the likes of Will Smith. Suddenly, the BET Awards show was a Thing, an Event, an honest-to-goodness award show, not quite on the level of the Grammys, but something of which I could be proud.

I was especially pleased with our cold openings, performances that were uniformly exciting and unexpected. In

2005, we managed to reunite the Fugees, and while their piece, a twelve-minute medley of their hits, was phenomenal, there was still a lot of lingering resentment within the group, so they didn't speak to each other, and were thus a nightmare to deal with, especially their spacey ingénue, Lauryn Hill. The only way we got Lauryn to sing with her old group in the first place was to give her a solo tune. Twelve minutes before she was scheduled to go on, the stage manager called me on my headset: "Lauryn won't come out of her dressing room."

I said, "Don't worry. We still have twelve, no, eleven minutes."

Two minutes later: "She's still in there."

"Don't worry. We still have nine, no, eight minutes."

Six minutes later: "Ron, she's still in her dressing room. Five minutes to stage."

"Okay, time to worry."

I sprinted to her room, where one of my co-producers was banging on her door, screaming, "Ms. Hill, three minutes! We need you! Now!"

Before I could take over the knocking, Lauryn's assistant opened the door and said, "Lauryn's tied up right now. Plus, she's not really inspired."

I said, "If she's not in the wings immediately, we're going to roll her set offstage and move on."

She didn't come out. We moved on. We had to. It was a live show, and I wasn't going to let a whack-job like Lauryn Hill derail us.

The rest of the show went off without a hitch, until we got to the closing act, Stevie Wonder. I was standing stage left, looking at the backward-running countdown clock, which told me how much time was left in the show. While Stevie ran through a medley of his hits, my stage manager told me, "Lauryn's in the wings, stage right. She's looking for you."

"Whatever. She knows where to find me."

And indeed she found me. With two minutes left in the show, she glided over, clad in a flowing white dress, clutching a piece of paper. "I'm ready to go on," she said.

"Lauryn, you can't. After Stevie is done, the show's over."

"That's great. Stevie and I are in the same cosmic plane."

What? "Listen, Lauryn, it's not gonna . . ."

She waved the paper in my face and said, "I wrote a poem that I'd like to read after Stevie is done performing."

My stage manager appeared behind Lauryn, and I could tell that it was taking him every ounce of control to keep from exploding in laughter. I pointed to the clock and said, "There's only two minutes left. There is no *after*."

"Then I'll read it now," she said as she headed toward the stage.

I grabbed her arm, and, as she fought me—and she was strong for a little girl—the stage manager finally lost it. "You," I told him, "quit laughing! And you," I told Lauryn, "calm down and stay here!" After another minute of tug-of-war, Lauryn finally gave up, took her poem, and flew back to Mars.

But that wasn't the worst. That came the next year.

It was important to me that the BET Awards be a credible entity, so I always made it a point to invite well-respected African-American entertainers, whether or not they were nominated for an award or had a film or album to hype.

For years, I tried to get Halle Berry to appear, to no avail. I don't know if she didn't identify with the show, or if she felt it wasn't a big enough event, but for whatever reason, she refused, and refused, and refused.

Eventually, it became Favor Time.

Favor Time had worked out well for us. Me making nice with a certain person who shall not be named led to a performance by Destiny's Child, which led to a performance by Beyoncé, which led to a performance by Alicia Keys, which led to a performance by Stevie, which led to really, really good ratings. After a while, it was considerably easier to get these artists on board, because word got out that if they played the BET Awards, they'd be treated like gold.

Word got back to Halle's people that we were a good place to be, so one year, while she was filming a movie up in Vancouver, she agreed to come onto the show. (Here's a dirty little secret: To entice her, she was nominated for an award, and to make certain she made it onto the show, the BET brain trust made sure she'd win.) "But," her manager told me, "she has to go on in the first hour because she absolutely has to be on a 7:00 flight back to Vancouver." We went on air at 5:00, Los Angeles time.

As far as I was concerned, she could go on any time she damn well pleased, so I told Stephen Hill, BET's president of music programming and specials, the plan. Stephen had a reputation as a meddler, but I'd never had any issues with him. He said, "That's great, Ron. First hour it is."

The afternoon of the show, I was going over our rundown, and, as is almost always the case with this show, the timeslot for a number of the acts had changed. (This happens all the time on live shows, and as long as everyone is on the same page, it isn't a big deal in the least.) I was perfectly fine with all the changes, except for one: The presentation of the award for which Halle had been nominated was rescheduled for hour two.

I tracked down Stephen, shoved the rundown in his face, pointed at Halle's new time, and said, "This isn't happening. This is not a discussion. This isn't what we committed to, and we're standing by our word."

Stephen said, "This isn't her show. It's my show."

I lost it. "This is bullshit! I put my ass out on the line! I called in I-don't-know-how-many favors to make this happen! She's giving out an award right at the top of the show, then she's accepting her own award exactly thirty minutes later, and then she's outta here!"

He repeated, "This isn't her show. It's my show. I make the decisions, not Halle Berry."

"Don't do this, Stephen. She's gonna leave."

"No, she won't."

"Yes, she will. She's working on a movie, and she has a flight, and that's it."

He said, "Then she won't win an award," and stomped off. Sure enough, Halle left at 6:00. Sure enough, someone else won her award.

Unfortunately, the press release with the list of award winners had already been written. And Halle was among the listed. Every time someone called to yell at me about that one, I told them to call Stephen.

This kind of crap went on all throughout my BET tenure, but the 2011 show, when Beyoncé, Alicia Keys, and Maxwell all went through last-minute, disrespectful scheduling sna-fus, was the final straw. BET's lack of professionalism and honor was hurting my reputation with people whom I sin-cerely liked, and it wasn't worth the paycheck. So after the show, I went to the production office and, very calmly, told Stephen Hill and John Cossette—who never had my back during any of these messes— "I'm done. This is all bullshit. You guys are full of shit. Fuck you. Goodbye."

John said, "Come on, Ron. Shit happens. Take a week. We'll talk then."

We didn't talk. And for me, it was the end of the BET story. But not for Stephen Hill. As of this writing, he's still there, still overseeing their Awards show. A number of artists who know what happened have told me that they appear on the show because they have to, but it's not the same without me, and that I'm correct in my assessment of Hill: He's a prick.

But that sort of crap is an anomaly; the vast majority of the time, production is fulfilling, and then some, especially when it comes to my old stomping grounds, the Apollo Theater. For the last decade or so, I've produced the annual Apollo Theater Hall of Fame concerts. Michael, Quincy, Gladys, James Brown, Smokey Robinson, Aretha Franklin, Lionel Richie, and Little Richard are among the inductees, but the most memorable, most magical night for me was Stevie Wonder's.

Like anyone else with a working set of ears, I love Ste-vie's music, but as great a musician as he is, he's an even better person. Tony Bennett, another class act, was invited to induct Stevie, and he accepted without a moment's hesitation. They'd performed together in the past, and their respect for one another was off the charts.

After Tony gave Stevie his award, Stevie stepped to the mic and said, "Thank you, Tony. I just want to remind everybody here tonight that before it was fashionable, this man was supportive of a lot of African-American musicians. When he was at the height of his popularity, he went out of his way to perform with Ella Fitzgerald, and Count Basie, and Duke Ellington, and Cab Calloway. He ignored the threats of blacklisting and worked with anybody he wanted to, regardless of race, creed, or color." He turned to Tony and said, "I might not be able to see the color of your skin, but I feel the color of your heart."

That day, Stevie was on a roll. Earlier in the afternoon, he met with Michael Whitaker, a twelve-year-old keyboard prodigy who'd won Amateur Night at the Apollo. Stevie was Michael's idol in part because if you liked soul music and you played piano, you couldn't help but idolize Stevie, and in part because he, too, was blind. I decided that Michael should open the show that night, because what better way to demonstrate Stevie's legacy?

After Michael's rehearsal, I brought him down to meet Stevie. Michael grilled his hero for a good twenty minutes, and Stevie was more than a little impressed, because Michael seemed to know everything about his career. Stevie then asked Michael a few somewhat complex questions about Stevie's songs, all of which Michael answered with authority. Steve was *really* impressed, because Michael was a walking Stevie Wonder encyclopedia. "I can't remember some of these things," Stevie said.

After some more back-and-forth, Stevie said, "What instruments do you play other than piano?"

Michael said, "Well, my focus is mostly on keyboards." He paused, then added, "My family doesn't really have enough money to get me any instruments."

"Did you ever want to play the harmonica?" Stevie asked.

Michael's eyes lit up. "Yeahhhhh! But I don't really have the time."

Stevie nodded, then reached into his pocket, took out his harmonica, and handed it to Michael. "I'll give you this if you promise to practice."

Immediately, tears rolled down Michael's face. Between that, and what Tony Bennett said about Stevie, that was one of the greatest days of my professional life, the kind of thing that makes it all worthwhile. Just like my night in Miami with Beyoncé Knowles.

The Miami Children's Hospital is one of the greatest entities with whom I've had the pleasure to be associated, because if you're a child with a life-threatening disease—if you have cancer, if you need an organ replaced, if you've contracted a disease that no one has figured out how to cure— they'll treat you at no cost. In order to keep their doors open, the MCH holds an annual fund-raising concert; in 2008, some friends asked me to meet with the hospital administration, in hopes I could produce that year's show. When he explained to me what MCH is about, I cleared my schedule.

Once down in Miami, I was given a two-hour tour of the hospital, but I didn't need two hours. Fifteen minutes into the walk-through, I said, "You guys are amazing. This place is amazing. I'm in. What do you need from me?"

The point person said, "We want to bring in a big chunk of money this year, so whatever we do, it has to be . . . " She trailed off.

"Big?" I said.

"Yes. Exactly. Big. We want to make a statement. First off, we need a big place to host it." After I reeled the names of some venues in Miami—two theaters, three hotels, all of which had a capacity in the vicinity of 3,000—she said, "Well, one of the people on our board runs the American Airlines Arena. Would that be something you could work with?"

The American Airlines Arena has a capacity of almost 20,000. It plays home to the Miami Heat, as well as the country's biggest of the big concert tours. I told her, "If we could fill it, that sure would make a big statement, wouldn't it?" I considered it for a second, then said, "How about we set up tables on the floor and make those seats available to the public, in addition to the ones in the stands? Then we come up with an artist to honor—maybe Beyoncé—and we have some other artists perform, and it'll be a great show." They loved it, Beyoncé signed on, and the wheels started turning.

While I was planning the show with the MCH brain trust, they introduced me to an eight-year-old piano prodigy named Ethan Bortnick. Ethan lived at the hospital because a couple years prior, he'd had a heart transplant, but that didn't stop him from playing some mean keyboard, even though his feet barely touched the pedals. I would've put him on the bill even before I heard him hit a single key, but once I saw him blow through a couple of tunes, it was a no-brainer.

A few weeks before the show, I sat down with Ethan and told him, "I have a couple of songs I'd like you to do. Let me know if you know them, or if you like them." As I showed him the sheet music for John Lennon's "Imagine," I said, "If you play this, we'll have the lyrics on a big screen at the back of the stage, and everybody will sing along, and it'll be great."

He read the lyrics, smiled, and said. "I'm gonna work on it with my piano teacher, so when I show up, I won't mess you up!"

I laughed, then said, "At the end of the show, after Beyoncé says what she wants to say about the hospital, I have another song for you. Would you like to play 'Over the Rainbow,' special for Beyoncé?" She'd just performed a brilliant version of the song at the Oscars, and I thought she'd get a kick out of it.

"I know that song! I'm gonna work on that one every day, too!" If all the artists I worked with had Ethan's drive, the world would be a better place to live.

The afternoon of the show, I pulled Beyoncé aside and told her, "There's going to be a little surprise for you at the end of the night. But it's nothing you need to be uncomfortable about. You know me, and you know I wouldn't put you in an awkward position."

She nodded. "I trust you. It's cool."

At the end of the evening, after Smokey Robinson performed, and Lucy Morillo, president of Miami Children's Hospital Foundation, presented Beyoncé with the award, she took to the podium and gave a touching speech about her own daylong visit to the hospital, then thanked the crowd for their generosity, after which Ethan came out to play "Over the Rainbow."

After the first chorus, Beyoncé walked over to the piano, and all she could do was stare. A few bars later, as Beyoncé stared at him with awe and compassion, Ethan said loudly enough so we could all hear, "I gotta get through this!" I don't know whether he was speaking to Beyoncé or himself. Regardless, it was a charming, touching moment.

He finished the song to wild applause, then, after doing the kind of cute, awkward bow that only an eight-year-old can pull off, he took the microphone and said, with complete confidence, "If you think that was something, wait'll you see this!"

The lights went out, and on the giant screen at the back of the stage, my tech crew fired up a tape of her Oscar performance. I was standing in the wings, so I was able to catch Beyoncé's eyes and mouth, "Surprise." She gave me the Beyoncé smile that made Jay-Z—and the rest of the world, for that matter—fall in love with her.

When the tape ended, Ethan launched right into "Imagine," and four bars in, I started getting goose bumps. I thought, *Here's a song written almost thirty years ago, and the lyrics are so impactful that they'll touch anyone of any age, in any country in the entire world. And even if you don't understand what the lyrics mean, the spirit and the melody alone will convey Lennon's message of peace, love, and understanding. And music is the only entity on this planet that can bring together this many people.*

And that's why I'm so proud that music is my life, and my life is music.

EPILOGUE

Music Biz 101:
A Primer for Up-and-Coming Musicians and Potential Managers

I have thousands of songs on my laptop. I think I have every record that Ella Fitzgerald ever cut in the studio, plus dozens of bootlegs. I have Basie, and Ellington, and Sinatra, all kinds of jazz material. And when I listen to the radio, or watch a music channel, or see an awards show, I'll sometimes see a fabricated band, or a singer warbling over a backing track, and think, *Who will this appeal to? And will anyone care about it three months from now?* And then there are the acts who do the same thing over and over and over.

If you want to transcend, you have to change and grow. You might be able to squeeze two similar albums out of someone without turning off a fan base, but if you want to have an actual career, *stretch*. There are, of course, exceptions to this—Green Day, for instance, has been making more or less the same album for almost twenty years, and they're doing okay. But for the most part, unless you mine your soul for diverse, heartfelt material, and hook up with a simpatico producer who has a vision of his or her own—and isn't burnt out from decades in the studio—you'll be one and done.

I always look for acts that have multiple wells of talent to draw upon. If you can sing but you can't perform, or

214

perform but not sing, or play an instrument but not play it well, I probably won't be interested in you, no matter how good-looking you might be. But if you can do it all—sing, dance, entertain—I'm interested.

Once you land a manager, and then a record deal, it's crucial to have a happy, successful marriage with your label. You have to get the label to commit to you, and that means going beyond making a great record. First off, you have to work in tandem with your A&R person. When the term was first coined, the A&R staff did just that: found the artists and picked their repertoire. As musicians became more creative, and as record label rosters became more bloated, A&R people did less artist and repertoire work and more babysitting, turning many of the creative duties over to the producer. Even if your A&R rep is completely removed from your recording process, you have to maintain a good relationship with him or her. If you push him away, or give him attitude, he'll disown your project, and for a project to go next level, you have to have the support of the label at every level, whether you're Michael Jackson or Joe Shmo.

Your project is far from over when the record is done—as a matter of fact, some would call it just the beginning, because publicity is almost as important as cutting a good record and putting on a good show. You have to make yourself available, both physically and emotionally, because if you alienate the publicity and marketing people, they're not going to be as interested in publicizing or marketing you. If you don't regularly show up on time and act professional whenever you're in public, and just generally be a good person, you'll put off your label, the press, and your fans. Plus, your manager might get fed up with you and take a hike.

And then there's the live show. If you're a good band, you've probably spent hours in a garage, or a rehearsal room, or your drummer's basement, so chances are you have the ability to put together sixty minutes of enjoyable live music. But—and this will be a theme throughout your musical life—you have to know how to entertain. Engage with the audience. Come up with some quality in-between-song banter. Bring your A-game to each club, each night, each song. Don't have someone walk away thinking they've just pissed away their hard-earned money. You have three goals at a live performance: (a) Make your listeners want to buy your record; (b) make your listeners tell their friends about how much they enjoyed the show; and (c) make your listeners want to come hear you play every time you come to their town. You might not be able to accomplish all three goals—some nights, it's just not there—but if you don't try, I probably won't want to work with you. If you're a singer who tours with a backing band, you must have the ability to not just re-create what you did in the studio but also improve on it. And if you aren't able to improve on it—and there's no shame in that—at least give the concertgoers something they didn't get on the record. (In that respect, Curtis Mayfield was my dream client. I never left one of Curtis's shows without hearing things like, "Man, his vocals were incredible," or "I had no idea he could play guitar like that," or "That guy can do it all." If I had a roster full of Curtis Mayfields, I might well still be managing today.)

You also must be patient. Some acts come out of the gate with the corporate machine roaring behind them, but for the most part, it's a slow build. Your first single might not pop, your shows might not sell out, and your fan base might wax and wane, but don't give up hope. Just keep working hard, keep writing great songs, keep giving terrific performances. Eventually, be it next month, next year, or next decade, chances are you'll find an audience. Maybe not a huge audience—not everyone is cut out to play Madison Square Garden—but an audience that will enable you to quit your office gig and make music for a living.

Also, it's essential to think long-term. The second you finish your current record, start writing music for the next one. Have a game plan, so you'll always have something to fall back on when you don't know what to do next. And get everyone on your team pointing in the same direction: your fellow musicians, your label, your management, your road crew, *everyone*. One dissenter can derail not just your current project but your project three projects down the line.

And now some thoughts for potential managers: A huge part of your job is figuring out a way to get your artists to step up, to go the extra mile, to recognize that music is a 24/7/365 job. Get them to say yes to anything and everything, no matter how inconsequential it may seem: a college radio interview, an acoustic in-store performance at an indie place in Nowheresville, Idaho, an autograph signing at a mall, the sort of thing that doesn't just make fans, but makes fans for life. And when they step up, you have to step up with them, to follow through, to be available, to innovate, to work your ass off. Because if you're not working your ass off, they'll have an excuse not to work their asses off.

Even if you follow this advice to a T, there's no guarantee you'll be able to sign any artist you want, nor is there a guarantee that once you sign that artist, he or she will succeed on a large scale . . . or, for that matter, a small scale . . . or, for that matter, any scale at all. There are a lot of great representatives out there, but the best ones aren't necessarily the biggest. Sometimes it's terrific to have the power of, say, CAA behind you, but other times, you're better off with a smaller team, a company where you can get more individual attention. And if you're in my position, you have to make your company a welcome landing spot, and, for that, you have to work tirelessly and develop a rock-solid reputation. But as long as you're honest, as long as you're respectful, as long as you always do what you say you're going to do, as long as you don't try to hustle someone just to get him or her in the door, you'll be more than okay. And that's what it's all about.

POSTSCRIPT

Here, Ron Weisner and his cowriter, Alan Goldsher—himself a former professional musician and record label executive—discuss the differences in music and the music business between then and now. And we all know what we mean by "then" . . .

AG: What with the Internet and TMZ, a celebrity can't do anything without someone eventually hearing about it. Based on Joe Jackson's shenanigans, I'm guessing that there used to be a lot of nefarious behavior behind the scenes.

RW: There was, but I wasn't afraid to stand up for myself when necessary. I'm sure there were times I was out of my mind to have done so. There were people around the country—the mafia, the urban mafia—who controlled venues, and if you weren't doing what they wanted you to do, and you were coming to their town, well, suffice it to say that I always traveled with a couple of LAPD guys who were licensed to carry weapons. One afternoon when an act of mine was playing in Providence, Rhode Island, one of my security guys told me, "I got a call from somebody who told me you can't go to the show tonight." I said, "Fuck that. I go anywhere I want. If you want to watch my ass, that's fine, but I'm going." That happened more than once, and it made me nervous, but never to the point where I thought about hiding out.

AG: Did you carry a gun?

RW: Yeah. On the road. Almost always. I even had to pull it a few times, usually in response to someone pulling their piece on me. They were almost always surprised that I wasn't some wuss who was going to stand there and take their shit.

AG: Do you think someone would've actually pulled the trigger, or were they just trying to intimidate you?

RW: Both. There were a couple instances where, if we weren't in a public place, bullets might've flown. But because there were people around, they didn't shoot, because they knew they wouldn't get away with it. You have to remember, if you were in the touring business, and you were taking money from someone—even if it was rightfully yours—you were the bad guy. I don't know anyone who got shot, but I know plenty of people who got worked over.

AG: Did you ever catch anyone ripping you off?

RW: Oh yeah. Joe Jackson used to send people on the road with us. He'd give them some cockamamie title, but their only job was to skim cash.

AG: I went on a tour where the tour manager was skim-
ming from the top. He got caught, and they threw him off
the tour bus in the middle of nowhere. He didn't get beaten
up, but if the timing was right, I bet it would've happened.

RW: It would've been nice if you could've handled it like
they do in Vegas. If you try to screw over the casino, they'll
take you out to the desert, and, well, enjoy your vacation.

AG: The record industry that you grew up with is dead. The
climate that allowed Buddah to thrive doesn't exist, and
probably never will. To me, A&R is the most affected part
of your typical major label.

RW: Artist and repertoire definitely doesn't mean as much
as it used to. Back in the day, record labels were willing to
work with managers to nurture and develop talent—your
team did its thing, and their team did their thing, and when
it popped, it *really* popped. Everyone spent the time, the
money, and the energy to break an act.

AG: True, but on a certain level, I can understand why what
few A&R people are left in the world are so gun-shy about
putting themselves out there. If they push to sign an act,
and put in the time and the label's money, and the group
tanks, they'll take the brunt of the blame. If that happens
on a semi-regular basis, they'll lose their job in a heartbeat,
and good luck finding another one.

RW: Not only that, but there's been a massive shift in the pecking order. A&R used to be at the top of the heap, followed by creative services—advertising, marketing, promotion—with business affairs on the bottom. Once the corporations bought out all the small labels and put them under their umbrella, it completely reversed, with the Suits on the top and the Creatives on the bottom. Back then, your A&R guy would sign you to a three- or four-record deal, and they'd put together a master plan for not just the first record but the second and third. They were interested in careers, not hits.

AG: *Oh, they wanted hits, too.*

RW: Okay, of course they did, but a career was just as important.

AG: *Which kind of begs the question, what's the main difference between the musicians of the present, and those of your management days?*

RW: The majority of the people I managed were either singers, instrumentalists, or singers who played an instrument. To them, the most important thing—even more important than their records—was their live performances. They took pride in their shows, and they never lip-synched or sang to a backing track. When they did a record, they didn't do it in their bedroom with a laptop. It was in a studio with live musicians, sometimes just a rhythm section, and sometimes a full-blown orchestra with strings and horns. It isn't a matter of, "Is it better music today or yesterday," but it's different. It's really, really different.

AG: Touring is also really, really different. I went on the road with a couple of mid-level bands, and we had decent tour buses, which we slept in at night, in order to save money on a hotel. I also went on a couple of van tours, where we slept on sofas. Today, it seems like it's all or nothing—either you're in a gold-plated private plane or a beat-up Volkswagen Jetta.

RW: Getting your big show from one city to the next is so expensive now, and the logistics involved are nuts.

AG: But let's say we're talking about a Beyoncé tour. If you're paying $200 per ticket to see her show, you want a show. Is it possible for someone like that to go out with a stripped-down band, and no pyrotechnics, and lower the ticket price? Bruce Springsteen, for instance, just has a band. His tickets are expensive, but not as expensive as other stadium acts.

RW: Everyone wears a different hat. The people who come to see Springsteen know what they'll be getting for their money: a no-frills, three-plus-hour night of great music, one song right after the other. The people who come to see Beyoncé—just like the people who used to see Michael Jackson—expect a full-blown production, with lights, and video screens, and costume changes, and dancers, and lasers, and they're willing to pay for it. Different types of shows for different tastes.

AG: Okay, two questions: First, let's say that Beyoncé, or someone like her, goes on the road with a Motown revue sort of band—a rhythm section, three horns, and three background singers—will that make for a better show? And second, if she does a show like that with more affordable tickets, will she reach a different audience?

RW: I'll answer your questions with a question: What do people want to see? Do they want the full production show or the stripped show? The public dictates, and in my experience, over the last decade or two, they've wanted *shows*. They want to go to the circus. They want the bells and whistles, but they want *quality* bells and whistles. Using five tons of pyrotechnics doesn't make for a better show unless they're used wisely. Have you been to shows where you feel like you've been cheated? Like the act didn't do what you expected, or they did what you expected and did it badly?

AG: Of course. We all have.

RW: That's right. I've gone to see people I admire who, earlier in their career, put on killer shows. Now they just walk through it. They don't perform.

AG: I think The Who sometimes falls into that category. Do you have any specific artists?

RW: I won't name any names, but I recently went to a show where the guy sang half of a song, then yelled, "Sing along!" and pointed the mic at the audience. Next song, same thing.

Before the next song, he started giving out roses, then more sing-along.

AG: I saw Al Green do something like that in 1990.

RW: And he still does that. But when he does sing, he sounds great.

AG: He sounded great then, too. And the crowd ate up the bit with the roses. Me, I was annoyed because I just wanted to hear him sing. Plus I was way in the back, and it's not like I was going to be getting a rose.

RW: At times, Aretha does that sort of thing. I love her, but sometimes her head is in a strange place. When's the last time you saw Earth, Wind & Fire?

AG: In 2011.

RW: They put on a great live show. Energy for days, music for days. They used to have big, big production, lights, sets, the works. At a certain point, their business people told them they couldn't afford to do that, and they cut out all the production.

AG: At the show I went to, it was some nice lighting and an American flag backdrop, and that was it.

RW: But their music is timeless. And the way they move onstage, and the way they work together, and the way they intertwine—they don't need anything.

AG: [EW&F bassist/co-founder] Verdine White is in his sixties, and he still moves like a kid.

RW: Energy-plus, that guy. That's why old fans who come to see them now aren't disappointed they aren't getting the show from twenty years ago. But you know what? If they cut their show down even more—if they went from, say, sixteen members to eight—I bet people wouldn't come back.

AG: So that being the case, you probably do think that once your show is a circus, it always has to be a circus.

RW: Some people need the pyrotechnics and some people don't. Springsteen is a *musician.* He's a different animal. He's an anomaly. There aren't any other acts of his generation who can still pull off a stadium show with musicianship. But it's not fair to compare his show to the flavor-of-the-month boy band's. It's a different animal. It's that simple. And then there's Britney Spears. What's that?

AG: It's Vegas with a backing track.

RW: It's horrible.

AG: It's embarrassing.

RW: As a consumer, would you feel ripped off if the entire show is on tape?

AG: Yes, but I'm a musician, so I'm looking at it from a different angle. I have a friend with a thirteen-year-old daughter who worships One Direction, and she wouldn't care if they farted their songs.

RW: There's a chance that by the time this book comes out, nobody's going to remember who One Direction is. Speaking of Vegas, they have some big-ass productions out there. Like Celine Dion at the Coliseum at Caesar's Palace. That's a Cirque du Soleil show that's been tweaked. She sings about 25 percent of the songs. Everything else, she synchs to a track. If someone feels like that's worth $250 a ticket to see that show—and there are a lot of people who feel that way—who am I to argue? But it's not all bad. You can go to see Carlos Santana at the Hard Rock, and you're getting nothing but music.

AG: True, but nobody will pay $250 to see that. That'll be a $35 ticket, tops. Which begs the question, why do you think that other than the Stones, there aren't any arena rock bands anymore? Even Foo Fighters don't play twenty-thousand-seat venues.

RW: This goes back to how this whole discussion started: money in most cases. If a promoter is going to make any money, the show has to sell out. If they do 85 percent to 90 percent capacity, they might break even. Anything below that, they lose money. Sometimes they'll book the show even though they know they'll take a loss just to maintain their relationship with the act or the act's management. Can

Foo Fighters fill stadiums all across the country? Maybe in some cities, but not everywhere. Promoters won't put their asses too far out there even with someone like Lady Gaga. They'll announce one show, then, if it sells out, depending on the public's interest, maybe they'll book another. Or maybe not. Because they don't know if she'll be relevant. And promoting shows is more difficult than ever. It used to be if a big artist went on a big tour, the *Rolling Stones* of the world would cover it from every angle. Now, the only way you get on a magazine cover is if there's a scandal or tragedy. But that doesn't matter much, because there aren't any magazines anyhow. Everything's online, and online content hasn't proven to have significant impact on ticket sales.

AG: So with big shows, no matter who it is, it's a crapshoot.

RW: It's a crapshoot from both ends. The acts are gambling as much as the promoters. To haul all those bodies and all the equipment around the world is an expensive proposition. The first thing I learned about touring was that it's very easy to spend money, and it's very hard to earn money. The Creatives want to add, and add, and add, and they get approval before anyone does the math. But then you run the numbers: You're on the road for eight months, you're doing ninety-one shows, and all this adding is bringing the costs up by eight grand a show. That could kill your bottom line. These days, one way they make it up is to sell VIP seats. Like you can shell out $2,500 to sit by the soundboard. Sell twenty of those, and you've covered your traveling party's lodgings for the night.

AG: Can you make it up with merchandise sales?

RW: You can, but you can't depend on it. It's out of your control.

AG: But you can control whether or not you have good merch.

RW: Sure, but that usually involves making some sort of licensing and manufacturing deal, and that costs, so you have to sell more shirts and hats, and that's another crapshoot. Plus if you're playing, say, the United Center in Chicago, and you want to sell your merch at the show, local unions dictate that you have to use their crew to move your stuff, and they get around 20 percent of your sales. So yes, there's money to be made on the road, but everyone has their finger in the pie.

AG: On the other hand, with bands on club tours, they survive on merch. If they don't sell any T-shirts or CDs, they might have to choose between eating and filling up their gas tank. So not only do you have to get people to come out, but also you have to get them to buy stuff on top of the cover charge and the drink minimum. It's like the disappearing middle class: You either drive from city to city in a luxury bus and stay at the Ritz, or you putter across the country in a shitty car and hope you can afford some fast food. Who do you blame?

RW: There is nobody to blame. That's the climate. The system is what the system is, and, at this point, it's nearly impossible to change it.

AG: In a way, we can blame Michael Jackson. He was one of the first pop acts to put on a heavily produced show. Before him, Queen, Led Zeppelin, and Styx were the kind of groups that filled stadiums. Most of them had some sort of production-oriented stuff—elaborate lighting, smoke machines, video projections, et cetera—but it wasn't anywhere near what Michael did, at least on the Thriller *tour.*

RW: Michael's shows were very, very expensive. He used to add, and add, and add. Effects, and costumes, and dancers—it was phenomenal. If he had a vision, and he wanted to do it, he'd do it.

AG: That makes sense, because you said that Michael was more about making history than money.

RW: Don't get me wrong: He wanted to make money, too. But if, say, he wanted to come up through the floor in the middle of the arena, it was going to happen, cost be damned. It got to the point that the show was so big, it was like moving a city. On Michael's first stadium tour, we needed twenty semis to haul everything. It took so long to set up that we needed two full sets and two full crews, so one crew could go ahead to the next city and get everything set up on time. Crew one would be with us in Pittsburgh on Monday, and crew two would be in Philadelphia, setting up for Thursday.

Then, when we finished in Pittsburgh, crew one would head to Washington so we'd be ready to go when we got there on Sunday. A lot of bodies, and a lot of gear.

AG: Were they so expensive that you didn't make any money?

RW: If you play enough shows, and you sell out every venue, every night, you make money. When I was working with McCartney, we had to scale down his US show in order to keep it profitable. In Europe, when he played "Back in the USSR," he had a fighter jet fly on a track from the back of the house to the stage, and then back again. When it was in the middle of the venue, the bomb bay doors opened, and out came thousands of peace leaflets. There was a whole separate crew responsible for making sure the plane went off without a hitch, and it cost him a fortune, but in Europe, the numbers worked out so that it was worth it to him. The States were a different story. He left the plane at home. I thought that was the wise decision.

AG: But Paul has more money than Fort Knox.

RW: True, but again, it was the wise decision. I didn't tell him to do that, mind you. I laid out the numbers, and he made the call. The only thing you can do as a manager is advise. You know who had a rude awakening with this kind of thing? Usher. And his manager at the time was his mother, Jonnetta Patton, a nice lady who wanted to do the right thing by her kid. Early on in her managerial career, she called me to get recommendations on production people. When she told me what Usher was looking to do for his stage show—and I guesstimated how much it would cost—I told her, "Listen, Jonnetta, you'd better make sure you lay out the costs for your son. If he thinks he's getting one figure, and he gets something that's considerably less, he's not going to be happy, whether you're his mother, his brother, or some schmuck off the street. Put it all in writing and show it to him, because you don't want him to come to you after the tour and say, 'Mom, what the fuck did you do?' You're steering the ship, and you don't want to hit an iceberg." Not too long thereafter, I heard that Usher fired her. What she didn't understand was that the manager has to have a complete overview of *everything* her artist is spending, because at some point, she's going to have to answer to him. If the act asks what he's spending on hotels, or per diem, or union fees, or sidemen, you have to have the answer right off the top of your head, or be able to get the answer in two minutes. Hey, guess which one of my acts *always* wanted to have all kinds of production shit, but *always* got bitchy about paying for it?

AG: Madonna.

RW: Madonna. Her shows were expensive to mount and move, and she's cheap, and wanted to nickel and dime everyone. When she'd tell the production manager what she wanted to do onstage, he'd go get a quote, then when he presented it to her, no matter what it was, she'd blow up: "That's ridiculous, I'm not gonna pay that, blah blah blah."

AG: So do you think later in her career, when she hired, say, Jean Paul Gaultier to do her costuming, she tried to get him on the cheap?

RW: Probably. That's the way she was. The Madonna I knew did whatever she could to get whatever she wanted, on her terms. And as I mentioned, there were very few things that she wasn't willing to do to get it.

AG: When you nickel and dimed on her behalf, did anyone ever say, "Screw you, this is Madonna we're talking about, so you're paying full price"?

RW: Sometimes. Some vendors didn't want to set a precedent, because if word got out, they'd get killed on everything. Some think they may as well, because as I've said throughout this book, something is better than nothing. Same with musicians.

AG: Tell me about it. When I was playing back in the '90s, I was rarely, if ever, able to negotiate more money, because there were a dozen great bass players just waiting by the phone who'd do the gig for less.

RW: You're right. Today, you'd be lucky to get paid what you got paid then. It's so hard to make it as a musician in this era. Unless you're independently wealthy—or unless your parents get tired of you talking about how hard it is to be an artist in today's world, and they give you a chunk of cash just to shut you up—I don't know how you'd survive.

The opportunities just aren't there. It was easier back then. There was more support, more of a sense of community. Look at a guy like Lewis Black, the comedian. I've paid to see him about fifteen times in the last two years, and he always has one of his old friends as his opening act. If musicians thought like that—if they remembered where it was they came from, and how they got to where they are—things would be better all around.

AG: Are things really that bad?

RW: You know what? As long as there's good music and good people—and there are, and there always will be—everything will be okay.

ACKNOWLEDGMENTS

Alan Goldsher: *I was fortunate to find someone who actually "got it." I can't emphasize enough what it was like spending a wonderful week in Chicago in the dead of WINTER.*

Lara Asher
Jim Gosnell
Steve Fisher
Corrine Plieth
Halston Mathis
Diana Villegas
Harrison Funk

INDEX

Italicized page numbers indicate photographs. Footnotes are noted with "n" after page number.

ABOUT THE AUTHORS

Ron Weisner began his career as a music manager in the '60s. Working at Buddah Records at a pivotal time, Weisner got to work with some of the most influential artists of the period, including Gladys Knight, Bill Withers, and Curtis Mayfield. He also managed Michael Jackson, Paul McCartney, Madonna, and myriad other superstar musicians. He has also spent decades producing television shows and special events. He produced fund-raisers for the 2008 Obama presidential campaign.

Alan Goldsher is the author of fourteen books, including the acclaimed Beatles/horror comedy *Paul Is Undead: The British Zombie Invasion.* As a ghostwriter, he has collaborated with numerous celebrities and public figures. For more information, visit www.AlanGoldsher.com.